Cherish Christ
Above All

The Bible in the
Rule of Benedict

DEMETRIUS DUMM, OSB

PAULIST PRESS
New York • Mahwah, N.J.

Also by Demetrius Dumm, OSB
published by Paulist Press

FLOWERS IN THE DESERT

Cover design by Frank Vitale.

Library of Congress Cataloging-in-Publication Data

Dumm, Demetrius, 1923–
    Cherish Christ above all : the Bible in the rule of Benedict /
Demetrius Dumm.
        p.   cm.
    Includes bibliographical references.
    ISBN 0-8091-3646-5
    1. Benedict, Saint, Abbot of Monte Cassino. Regula. 2. Benedictines—
Rules. 3. Benedictines—Spiritual life. 4. Bible—Use. 5. Bible—Influence.
I. Title.
BX3004.A2D85 1996
255'.106—dc20   96-4740
                                                                              CIP

Published by Paulist Press
997 Macarthur Boulevard
Mahwah, NJ 07430

Printed and bound in the
United States of America

Contents

TO MY PARENTS
ESTHER AND GORDON
WHO MODELED FOR NINE CHILDREN
THE MEANING OF GENTLE WISDOM
AND DEEP FAITH
"Love and the gentle heart
are one same thing" (Dante)

Foreword

I have named my book *Cherish Christ Above All* because these words from Saint Benedict's Rule (chap. 5:2) capture the essential element in his understanding of Christian monastic spirituality. The two central chapters of my book explain how Christians experience the love of the Father through Christ and are thereby empowered to share that love with others, also through Christ. In this way, a deeply personal and loving union with Christ is the cornerstone of Benedict's spirituality, and he certainly made this discovery through a faith that was nurtured by his daily pondering and praying of the scriptures.

Very few would question the influence of scripture on the Rule of Benedict. The very fact that he cites or alludes to the bible some 572 times should be proof of that. It is not my intention to analyze each and every one of these biblical references. Rather, I shall be concerned with the degree to which the biblical view of reality influenced Benedict's own vision of life. In other words, I shall be asking whether Benedict's spirituality is essentially biblical or whether the bible was simply cited, as has happened frequently, to support some other agenda.

Not surprisingly, I have concluded that Benedict's spirituality is biblical to the core. For this reason, I have not hesitated to cite biblical texts not found in the Rule, but related to Benedict's quotations, in order to flesh out, as it were, the bare bones of certain elements of Benedict's spiritual vision.

I have judged this procedure to be not only legitimate but necessary in order to uncover the riches of a Rule which was not written, after all, as a treatise on spirituality.

Since Benedict's wisdom is concerned with how to be a good Christian, as well as a good monastic person, I have attempted to suggest the importance of his guidance for those also who have not taken monastic vows. After all, the Rule of Benedict is not some esoteric teaching intended for an elitist group in the church. Rather, it is about living in the presence of God and in union with Christ—a matter of deep concern for all Christians. Benedictines simply attempt to live these common Christian realities in a more intense manner. Moreover, they do this for the sake of the church and not just for private satisfaction. Accordingly, the essential elements of Benedictine spirituality can be lived by every Christian, and it is my hope that this book will help to make that more evident.

Readers will also notice that I have made a conscious effort to use inclusive language throughout this book. It is true, of course, that Benedict had monks in mind when he wrote his Rule, and I have not attempted to revise his text. However, since most Benedictines in the world today are women, it seemed only proper to use inclusive language wherever possible. With this in mind, I have followed the practice of some recent authors who use the word "monastic" as a noun which, being gender neutral, would include monastic women as well as men. I have also chosen the inclusive language text of the New Revised Standard Version for biblical citations.

Citations from the Rule are taken from *RB1980: The Rule of Benedict*, except where noted. In identifying these citations, I have used "RB" for the Rule of Benedict and "Prol" for references to the Prologue of the Rule.

Finally, I wish to express my profound gratitude to Bishop Nicholas Dattilo of the Diocese of Harrisburg for generous support. I am deeply grateful also to the Sisters of St. Benedict's Convent in St. Joseph, Minnesota, who provided a loving and encouraging environment for writing in their Studium during the fall of 1994. Finally, I am grateful to my abbot, Douglas Nowicki, O.S.B., who steered me toward this project, as well as to my confrere, Campion Gavaler, O.S.B., for helpful comments, and to all my confreres, family and friends whose support has been unobtrusive but indispensable.

1

The Heart of Benedict's Rule

"What page, what passage of the inspired books of the Old and New Testaments is not the truest of guides for human life?" (RB 73:3).

Before we begin to consider how Benedict's spiritual vision grew out of his understanding of the bible, it may be helpful to discuss certain matters that will enable us to locate Benedict in the stream of Christian tradition. First of all, a few words must be said about the *text* of the bible available to Benedict. Then we will need to deal with the critically important matter of biblical *interpretation* and, in particular, the new light that modern scholarship casts upon the monastic way of reading scripture. Finally, some observations will be made about the *sources* of Benedict's teaching.

BENEDICT'S BIBLE

We know that the bible was written mostly in Hebrew (Old Testament) and Greek (New Testament). Benedict probably did not know either of those languages. His bible was a Latin translation. However, there were two principal Latin versions in use in Italy at the time of Benedict (born 480). St. Jerome (died 420) had already completed his monumental work (part translation and part revision) which would become the bible of the Western church for the next one thousand years. This translation came to be known as the Vulgate (or popular) version. Prior to Jerome, there was a Latin translation, called the Old Latin version, which dated from the second century. The Vulgate supplanted the Old Latin text eventually but this was a gradual process.

At the time of Benedict, the Old Latin version was still in common use and this is, in fact, the text represented in two-thirds of the biblical citations in the Rule. The remaining one-third would be from the Vulgate text. Since Benedict quotes the psalms more than any other book of the bible, it should be noted that the text he used was the Roman psalter which was probably from the Old Latin version. (The Vulgate psalter was Jerome's translation which, because it was popular in Gaul [modern France], came to be known as the Gallican psalter.)

It may be of interest to note also which biblical books Benedict favored and how often he quotes them. According to scholars, Benedict's favorite Old Testament book was the book of Psalms, quoted 51 times, followed distantly by Proverbs, quoted just 9 times. In the New Testament, the letters of Paul are cited 29 times, while Matthew's gospel (used most often in the liturgy) is quoted 15 times. Frequently, Benedict does not quote directly but alludes to biblical texts by weaving them into his own composition. Thus, there are in the Rule only 64 direct quotations from the New Testament but 135 allusions. There are 141 direct quotations from the Old Testament and 232 allusions. These statistics are of importance primarily to show how profound was the influence of the bible on Benedict's Rule.

The clear impression given by this weaving of biblical passages into the text of the Rule is that of a person who was immersed, as it were, in the sea of scripture. Benedict also insisted that his followers study the bible every day:

"In the time remaining after Vigils (the night office), those who need to learn some of the psalter or readings should study them" (RB 8:3). By "study" Benedict meant something quite different from what we might think today. For him, it meant to memorize those portions of the bible which were especially useful for community prayer. This was particularly true of the psalter, but other texts were to be committed to memory also, as is evident from the following passages: "...there follows a reading from the Apostle (Paul) recited by heart" (RB 9:10) and "This (reading from the Old Testament) is to be recited by heart" (RB 10:2).

Then there are the many references in the Rule to *lectio divina* or "prayerful reading" (as it is aptly translated in *RB1980*). For example, "...the brothers should have specified periods for manual labor as well as for prayerful reading" (RB 48:1). "From the fourth hour (10:00 A.M.) until the time of Sext (noon), they will devote themselves to reading" (RB 48:4). And, finally, "Then after their meal they will devote themselves to their reading or to the psalms" (RB 48:13). Moreover, older members are to be assigned the task of seeing that the younger ones are not distracted from this important duty (RB 48:17-20).

This "prayerful reading" of the scriptures was not just for familiarity through memorization, much less for mere information. Rather, it was a slow, deliberate and meditative murmuring of the sacred text with generous pauses to allow for prayerful response to the word of God. The end result of years of such prayerful reading was a monastic person whose subconscious was so filled with biblical words and phrases that they would bubble to the surface on the slightest invitation. Benedict was, therefore, a truly "biblical man," and he expected his followers to be similarly imbued with the holy scriptures.

NEW LIGHT ON BIBLICAL HERMENEUTICS

Anyone who has paid much attention to biblical studies will be aware that one of the most vibrant areas of research in recent years has been concerned with the best methodology for the interpretation of biblical texts. This field of studies is also called hermeneutics, from the Greek deity Hermes, who was considered the messenger and interpreter of the gods.

As might be expected, Benedict followed the methodology that was in vogue in the early patristic period. This approach was profoundly influenced by the great scholar Origen, and was typical of the Alexandrian school. The most notable feature of this method was its strong emphasis on the *spiritual* sense of scripture, that is, on a meaning that benefited from the light of faith and which, therefore, transcended the literal or obvious meaning. Such a methodology began with the assumption that the bible was the word of God and that, as such, it could have meanings that were quite possibly unknown to its human author.

One can well imagine that such a methodology could easily lead to arbitrary interpretations since it is very difficult to determine which interpreter is guided by authentic faith. For this reason, modern scholars, who are committed to rigid scientific methods, generally dismiss patristic interpretation as pre-scientific, which is simply a kind way of saying subjective and unreliable.

However, for those who take the trouble to study this early exegesis, it becomes clear that the early monastic and patristic interpreters were generally quite respectful of the literal meaning of the text. Their principal problem was that they lacked the means for examining the literal sense and therefore were often inclined to seek a spiritual sense because the literal meaning was unclear or made no sense.

As far as Benedict is concerned, he is remarkably sober

and circumspect in his interpretation of scripture. For example, there are only about ten instances in the Rule where the so-called accommodated sense is used. This occurs when the application of the text has only an apparent relationship to its original meaning. An example of this is Benedict's use of Psalm 66:12: "...you (God) let people ride over our heads." In the literal meaning of this text, the reference is to enemies who have oppressed Israel. Benedict gives this text an altogether different meaning when he writes: "Then, to show that we ought to be under a superior, (scripture) adds: 'You have placed men over our heads.'" Such an application has, of course, no relationship to the original meaning.

Where the interpreters of Benedict's day were weakest, modern biblical scholarship is very strong. It has produced biblical texts which are far more accurate than any of the Greek or Latin classics. Moreover, the modern historical-critical method has clarified the various literary forms used when the bible was written and has illuminated the historical and sociological context of those distant times. No one should ever want to return to the bad old days of corrupt texts and a biblical world that was poorly understood. A recent Vatican document, *The Interpretation of the Bible in the Church*, leaves no doubt about the position of the Catholic Church: "The historical-critical method is the indispensable method for the scientific study of the meaning of ancient texts" (p. 5).

However, for all its brilliant achievements, modern critical study of the bible has proved to be disappointing in some very important ways. It has illuminated the literal sense but it has neglected or denied the spiritual sense which was so important for the interpreters of Benedict's time. In the heady days of the enlightenment, it was thought that reason had at last been delivered from the bondage of faith and that scholars were now finally free to pursue the truth in a scientific and objective or unprejudiced way. Unfortunately, an objectivity that may be possible in the experimental procedures of the natural sciences is not so easy to achieve in a literary document like the bible. There was, of course, real need of better methods for biblical interpretation. The bible, however, being a book written by believers for believers, cannot be subjected to a methodology which may be appropriate for physics but which cannot in principle allow the possibility of a transcendent world.

Modern scientific interpretation of scripture has begun to discover its limits and, as it does so, the rich heritage of the monastic and patristic era is being rediscovered. A methodology is being developed that not only establishes the validity of the spiritual sense of scripture but provides effective safeguards against a subjective or arbitrary interpretation of the sacred text.

This new methodology has developed out of the work of scholars such as Paul Ricoeur and Hans-Georg Gadamer who were concerned with the way in which all significant texts speak to future generations of readers. They noted that every reader approaches the text from a world that differs from that of the author. According to modern critical scholarship, contemporary readers must try to detach themselves from their own world in order not to prejudice their understanding of the author's world. However, just the opposite seems to be true. For only by beginning with a deep understanding of their own real world can modern readers have any hope of communicating with the real world of the author. The true meaning of the text will be found only in a dialogue between the world of the reader and that of the author. Moreover, when the text resonates, as it were, in the world of the reader, it will reveal meanings that are in line with but go beyond the meaning of the original author.

The reader must, however, be truly in touch with his or her world in order to engage successfully in this dialogue.

The text will yield its riches of meaning only to those who have learned to abandon the world of illusions in favor of a world of truth and sincerity. Faith plays an essential role in this process because only believers can see the entire reality, transcendent as well as secular. Since the biblical author speaks from a world that assumes the reality of the transcendent or divine sphere, the reader who wishes to understand the full message of the author must also live in such a world.

In applying this hermeneutical methodology to the bible, scholars like Sandra Schneiders *(The Revelatory Text)* point out that faith, far from being a hindrance, is actually the indispensable condition for a full understanding of the text. This must, of course, be a mature and realistic faith that has been tested by the tradition from which it comes and in which it is lived. In such cases, the believer in future generations brings ever new questions to the biblical text and can expect to find answers that go beyond what the original author could have understood. This would be a classic example of the author saying more than he or she knew. This new meaning may indeed go beyond the original meaning but it can never totally disagree with it.

In this way, the tyranny of a so-called objective and scientific interpretation is replaced with a respect for the historical-critical method but with equal respect for the role of faith in the interpretation of the bible. The happy consequence is an interpretation that is based on good scholarship but that recognizes the deeper riches of the text and thereby provides a spiritual nourishment that scholarship alone cannot offer.

Such an interpretation of scripture, by blending the contributions of both reason and faith, also has the happy effect of undercutting the position of fundamentalist interpreters. For the primary justification offered by fundamentalists for their rejection of critical interpretation is that it seems to destroy the foundation for a traditional, believing and spiritually nourishing approach to the text. Now, however, it is quite possible to demonstrate the need for both a critical study of the bible, which would correct erroneous and naive understandings, and a deeper, spiritually richer interpretation drawing upon the vision of faith.

This reality has been confirmed by my personal experience as a professor of scripture in our seminary. When I finished graduate studies at the Ecole Biblique de Jerusalem, I felt competent to approach my task of biblical interpretation in a proper scholarly fashion. However, when I experienced the concrete reality of a classroom full of students who would soon need to proclaim and explain the biblical text, I recognized the need to do the scientific project but also to suggest to them how their faith and the faith of their future audiences could illuminate and enrich these words of life.

It should be obvious, of course, that the faith which can thus illuminate the sacred text is not a merely superficial overlay of traditional and largely verbal loyalties that leave secular attitudes quite intact. Authentic faith not only recognizes the value of biblical words but also embraces the implications of the saving events which are served by those words and which constitute the essence of biblical revelation. These saving events are the exodus of God's chosen people from the bondage of the pharaoh in the Old Testament and the definitive liberation of all people in the Easter event of Jesus, Son of God. Mature faith enables us to embrace these saving events and to adapt our lives to their implications, namely, that true freedom comes from receiving the love of God (often channeled through humans) and that such freedom is solely for the purpose of loving others—an unselfish project that will bring suffering but also resurrection.

Believing on this level of personal conversion is possible only where there is personal honesty or integrity. Living in the illusion of self-sufficiency or the arrogance of intellectual sophistication does not open the door to fruitful interpretation. As the earlier mentioned Vatican document notes: "Access to a proper understanding of biblical texts is only granted to the person who has an affinity with what the text is saying on the basis of life experience" (p. 21). In a word, embracing one's real life in honesty and humility is a pre-condition for the faith that gives access to the great saving events of God in human history.

This approach also establishes the significance of the liturgical rites by which these saving events are made sacramentally present to every generation of believers. In this sense, the eucharist and the bible are a perfect match. And it is encouraging to see Catholics beginning to appreciate the table of the word as well as the table of the eucharist. Likewise, many Protestants are also recognizing that sacramental worship, based on biblical events, gives fuller meaning to the words of scripture.

MONASTIC HERMENEUTICS

Benedict inherited a biblical interpretation typical of the monastic tradition. This tradition has not been much appreciated by modern biblical scholars. However, as noted earlier, this view seems to be changing as the inadequacies of the historical-critical method become more apparent. The earliest monastics were devoted to the bible and were convinced that it was a sacrament of God's presence in their lives. It was, therefore, a constant challenge calling them to embrace reality, and thereby to be converted from the illusions and distortions that can prevent their proper entertainment of God's presence.

Douglas Burton-Christie has pointed this out convincingly in his recent book, *The Word in the Desert: Scripture and the Quest for Holiness in Early Christian Monasticism*. He sees the desert monastics of Egypt as apt exponents of the interpretation described by Ricoeur and Gadamer. For these monks and nuns often spoke of being "pierced to the heart" by the biblical word. They understood that the world of the bible made serious and personal demands on their own world. Moreover, they recognized that it was their humility and faith that made them so vulnerable to the demands of the biblical vision. They had no knowledge of scientific methods but they were strong where modern studies are often weak, namely, in the actualization of the text in their personal lives.

In this way, the biblical text was allowed to achieve its true purpose which is the holiness of its readers. As Burton-Christie puts it: "Holiness in the desert meant giving concrete shape to this world of possibilities stretching ahead of the sacred texts by interpreting them and appropriating them into one's life" (*The Word in the Desert*, p. 20). In other words, the text continues to speak to each succeeding generation and thereby challenges them to discover the meaning of salvation here and now rather than in some safe study of the past.

In this regard, we are reminded of the discussion between Jesus and the Pharisees in chapter 9 of John's gospel. The curing of the blind man by one who "broke" the sabbath created a dilemma for the Pharisees. They attempted to evade the implications of this miracle by appealing to Moses against Jesus: "We know that God has spoken to Moses, but as for this man, we do not know where he comes from" (v. 29). They had edited and "massaged" the torah into compliance with their prejudices but Jesus was the present and actual witness to God. By rejecting him, they were confirmed in blindness. These Pharisees (and all their modern counterparts) were willing to discuss endlessly the meaning of the safely distant world of Moses. However, when Jesus challenged their present and immediate world, they had to choose between safe argumentation and personal conver-

sion. Their choice was a tragic one. And so the biblical word
continues to pierce us to the heart, on condition that we
allow it to penetrate our well-guarded inner sanctuary. Only
real faith can cause this to happen.

It is this very personal understanding of the role of scripture that we find in the Rule of Benedict. Benedict almost
invariably personalizes the biblical text to show that it
speaks directly to one's contemporaries and not just to
people of the biblical era. We read in the Prologue to the
Rule: "Let us get up then, at long last, for the Scriptures
rouse us when they say: 'It is high time for us to arise from
sleep' (Rom 13:11)" (v. 8). Benedict clearly understands that
these words are addressed to himself and his followers,
indeed to all human beings, and not just to the first century
Christians of Rome.

This same challenging actuality is seen in the next verse
of the Prologue: "Let us open our eyes to the deifying light
and with thunderstruck ears let us hear the voice from
heaven that every day calls out this charge: 'If today you
hear his voice, harden not your hearts' (Ps 95:8)" (v. 9) (my
translation). This is one of Benedict's favorite biblical texts
as evidenced by his requirement that it be recited in the
monastery every day at the beginning of the night office
(RB 9:3). For he saw that faith is effective and conversion is
possible only when we dare to become vulnerable to the
challenge of the word of God in our lives.

That vulnerability will mean different things in each situation as new questions about the meaning of salvation are
brought to the biblical text. In Benedict's day, there were
questions about the possibility of living in peace and harmony in a disintegrating society. Today we must ask about
the possibility of trust and peace in a world full of violence
and fear. In this way, the lives of monastics should be examples of how the ancient biblical word of God can be
made dynamic and fruitful in every age.

BENEDICT'S SOURCES

There can be no doubt that the bible itself was the primary source of Benedict's spiritual teaching. He makes this clear when he refers to outside influences in the final chapter of the Rule. "What page, what passage of the inspired books of the Old and New Testaments is not the truest of guides for human life?" (RB 73:3). It may be worth noting that in this text he declares the scriptures to be the source of wisdom for all human lives and not just for the lives of monastics.

Next after scripture, Benedict cites the Catholic tradition: "What book of the holy catholic Fathers does not resoundingly summon us along the true way to reach the Creator?" (RB 73:4). This reference seems to suggest that Benedict was well aware of the danger of heretical positions during this period of rampant Arianism. Note again that the fathers are recommended for the guidance of all Christians and not just for monastics.

There was also a long and rich monastic tradition that preceded Benedict and he made full use of the wisdom of his predecessors. The Christian monastic movement originated at least two hundred years before him and it first appeared in the east, particularly in Egypt. The primary link between this Egyptian monasticism and the west was John Cassian who was born about a century before Benedict and to whose *Conferences* and *Institutes* Benedict refers explicitly in the same chapter 73 (RB 73:5). Other important influences were Basil and Augustine. (For a full discussion of these influences, see *RB1980*, pp. 3-64.)

Although Benedict gladly received the monastic tradition that preceded him, he did not leave it unchanged. First of all, he moderated the monastic way of life so that it would be accessible to ordinary mortals and not just to the heroes of the Egyptian desert. He also centered monastic spirituality in Christ in a way that was unprecedented. If the abbot plays a decisive role in the Benedictine community, it is because he models for that community a union with Christ that is to be the primary goal of their own spiritual journey.

In reflecting on the sources of Benedict's Rule, there is, finally, the fascinating question of the relationship between this Rule (RB) and the "Rule of the Master" (RM). This anonymous document, three times as long as the RB, contains passages that are identical with parts of Benedict's Rule. For centuries, it was assumed that the RM was written after Benedict's time and simply borrowed from his Rule. Now, however, "the weight of the evidence is definitely in favor of the priority of RM, and there is no longer any prominent expert in the field who holds that the RB is earlier than its sister rule" (*RB1980*, 72).

We must conclude, therefore, that Benedict borrowed from the RM substantial and significant parts of his Rule, notably in the critical doctrinal portion from the Prologue to chapter 7. It is truly amazing that he should have done so without ever mentioning this source, particularly since he does refer to other sources, as we have seen. The most obvious solution to this puzzle is the suggestion that Benedict himself is the author of *both* the RM and the RB. In fact, this solution was proposed already by Odo Zimmermann in the very first issue of the *American Benedictine Review* (pp. 11-36).

Adalbert de Vogue, the foremost scholar on the Rule of Benedict today, has concluded moreover that the RM was probably written at a time and place that would coincide precisely with the early years of Benedict. The major difficulty with this proposal seems to come from the nature of the RM which has some features that one would prefer not to ascribe to the great and holy Benedict. For the RM is characterized in places by tedious repetitions, by an insensitivity bordering on crassness and by frequently suspicious attitudes. It tries to provide for all possible situations whereas Benedict wisely leaves much to the discretion of future superiors.

Nonetheless, evidence is mounting in favor of an identification of the author of the RM as the youthful Benedict. A recent significant work favoring this view is *Regla del Maestro—Regla de S. Benito* by Ildefonso Gomez. Moreover, de Vogue himself seems to be edging toward this conclusion, for he has written recently: "Might (Benedict) have written this text (RM) himself—a text so seriously defective in some respects, but so remarkable in many others, during the early half of his career?" (*Reading St. Benedict: Reflections on the Rule*, p. 12).

It should be noted, finally, that the characteristics of the RM are exactly what one might expect from a young person who is idealistic but inexperienced and perhaps impulsive. By contrast, the Rule of Benedict would reflect the views of an older, wiser and more realistic author. In this case, recognizing a youthful Benedict as author of the RM would also show how he was able to change as he imbibed the wisdom of the scriptures and responded to the challenges of life— all under the guidance of the Spirit. Such an ability to undergo true conversion would, in fact, significantly enhance the stature of the great and holy Benedict and make him an even better model for Christians of every age.

2

God's Gracious Call

*"What...is more delightful than this voice
of the Lord calling to us?"* (Prol 19).

God has always been experienced by humans as one
who calls. Creation itself began with the divine command
that released light from darkness and order from chaos.
Nothing antedates God's gracious call. In fact, the existence
of an eternal Word of God, as revealed in the prologue of
John's gospel, suggests that God found speaking to be a
necessity of divine nature. Divine goodness could not help
reaching out and, as it were, speaking itself. Such goodness
simply cannot be contained.

Since this overture comes from the inexhaustible goodness of God, the call will not only summon being into existence but will also challenge all the forms of evil that may
later infect that good creation. "The light shines in the darkness, and the darkness has not overcome it" (Jn 1:5). In
other words, that divine call will invariably address all the
many forms of human oppression as it orders the severing
of bonds and the removal of unjust strictures. All of scripture, therefore, is about the reality of God's call and the possibility of our freedom.

The discovery of this reality constitutes the essence of
divine revelation. Israel learned this in that creative moment
of liberation from the bondage of Egypt and the Christian

community learned it in that definitive liberation that began on Easter morning. Accordingly, God is, first and foremost, the one who calls to freedom. Small wonder then that the Rule of Benedict should revel in the recognition of that fact, calling it delightful beyond compare: "What is more delightful than this voice of the Lord calling to us?" (Prol 19). The unspoken answer is that nothing in our experience can possibly bring more joy than God's gracious call, heard and savored in the depth of our being.

A PERSONAL ADDRESS

In reading the Rule, one cannot fail to be struck by Benedict's tendency to personalize most references to scripture. In only 15 out of 109 biblical citations does Benedict use the standard introduction: it is written. He chooses instead to present scripture as a personal address to the hearer: "...for the Scriptures rouse us when they say..." (Prol 8), or "...the voice from heaven that every day calls out this charge..." (Prol 9), or, again, "Brothers, divine Scripture calls to us, saying..." (RB 7:1). Such language reveals a person who knows that God is still reaching out in a loving, caring way. The biblical words are thus perceived to be present and actual and profoundly personal.

Benedict was well aware, therefore, that scripture is not just a collection of ancient words that somehow echo or resonate in the present. He and his contemporaries seem to have understood better than many more scholarly interpreters that there is a certain timeless quality to the words of scripture. This realization is based on an intuitive grasp of the profound sacramental nature of God's action in human history. All of God's decisive acts, whether it be creation, exodus or resurrection, have indeed a dated, historical aspect but, beyond that, there is an eternal and timeless dimension because divine activity simply cannot be limited by time and space.

This accounts for the deeper, symbolic meaning of scripture which presupposes the historical event but which transcends it. As pointed out in Chapter 1, this richest meaning of scripture is the first casualty of an interpretation which clings doggedly to the literal or historical sense. Discovery of the literal meaning is, of course, an essential first step but it must be left open to a deeper, symbolic interpretation. Therefore, when Benedict portrays God speaking in scripture directly to us in a vital and immediate way, he is distancing himself from a reading of scripture that is so scientific that it fails to recognize the perennial actuality of the presence of God in human history.

JESUS IS CALLED IN BAPTISM

We know, of course, that Jesus, as Son of God, was called from all eternity. However, the historical call to his mission of salvation is described in the gospel accounts of his baptism. The simplest and most ancient version of this story is found in Mark 1:9-11. Only one verse is needed to describe the actual baptism, and it is a model of literary economy: "In those days Jesus came from Nazareth of Galilee and was baptized by John in the Jordan."

In Matthew's version of this story, John the Baptist is said to have protested: "I need to be baptized by you, and do you come to me?" (Mt 3:14). Jesus insisted and John relented. This exchange is of some importance because it alerts us to the fact that this baptism of John was not solely for removal of sin. It had a positive aspect also because it included an earnest plea for God's intervention to bring about a new exodus. It did involve the issue of sin, but that was secondary, and meant simply that they wished to renounce any sinfulness that might still be an obstacle to the divine intervention. Jesus gladly joined the people in making this plea and in that sense it was entirely appropriate that he too should be baptized.

Most of Mark's story is devoted to what happened after the baptism itself. "And just as he was coming up out of the water, he saw the heavens torn apart and the Spirit descending like a dove on him" (1:10). It is remarkable that the heavens are said to have been "torn apart," and not just opened. This strong and unusual expression reminds us of the words of Isaiah, where the prophet makes an urgent plea to God for the people of Israel: "Oh that you would tear open the heavens and come down, so that the mountains would quake at your presence—as when fire kindles brushwood and the fire causes water to boil" (64:1-2). There too the plea is for the upheaval and transformation of a new creation. The heavens are torn open from God's side as God eagerly responds to Israel's pleading now that the chosen messiah is present with his people.

The parted clouds permit the passage of the Spirit in the likeness of a dove. This is highly symbolic language. It is meant to say in imagery that God's creative Spirit is active anew just as when it hovered over the deep in the original story of creation (Gn 1:2) or when it took the form of a dove to signal to Noah the beginning of a new era after the flood (Gn 8:11). The baptism declares, therefore, that God's creative power is once again active in a way that will change the world forever. Jesus is at the center of this new creation.

The climax of the scene comes with a revelation from on high. "And a voice came from heaven: 'You are my Son, the Beloved; with you I am well pleased'" (1:11). These dramatic words reveal the nature of this new creation. It will be effected through a new and limitless infusion of divine love. The words themselves are not original; they are a composite of words from Psalm 2:7, declaring the sonship of the royal messiah, and from Isaiah 42:1, foreshadowing a suffering servant who will die for his people. In effect, Jesus is declared to be the embodiment of that divine love and thus the center of the new world which that love envisions and makes possible.

BAPTISM IS FOREVER

Those divine baptismal words must not be understood as a single statement during a private episode at the beginning of the ministry of Jesus. They represent in fact a summary of all the divine affirmations of Jesus from birth to resurrection. As is the case with the temptation story which follows immediately, these experiences are merely the first in a series of such moments in the life of Jesus. Just as the temptations continued to the end, so does the affirmation accompany Jesus and was surely reinforced in those many encounters between Jesus and his heavenly Father as he withdrew from the disciples to be alone in prayer. All the freedom and strength of Jesus as a human being derived from this continuous experience of being empowered by God. And this was experienced until the end—indeed, especially at the end. These words were heard at Gethsemane far more clearly than on the banks of the Jordan.

If the baptismal experience of Jesus had implications for his whole life, it is true also that it is not at all restricted to his life. It is safe to say, in fact, that the evangelists were simply not interested in the private history of Jesus. If they were, they would surely have given us a description of his appearance. This story, like all the gospel stories, is preserved primarily for its symbolic value as a model for all the followers of Jesus in all times and places. All human beings who hope to find salvation in Jesus must yearn for God's intervention and must be ready for the changes of a new creation and, above all, must hear in their hearts those (paraphrased) liberating and energizing words: "You are my beloved child; I love you very much." There can be no real journey of salvation for any individual who has not had this baptismal experience. And, as should be obvious, going through a ritual baptism in infancy is in no way an adequate appropriation of this indispensable experience in and with Jesus.

BAPTISMAL CATECHESIS AND PSALM 34

We may surely assume that Benedict understood the importance of this baptismal experience, for he lived at a time when adult baptism was still common and he certainly was aware of the tradition which recognized monastic profession as a second baptism. Moreover, it has long been noted that there are elements of baptismal catechesis in verses 14 to 17 of the Prologue where Benedict comments on Psalm 34:12-18. In this context, then, monastic profession would be viewed as a deepening and strengthening of the original Christian experience of baptism.

When we look at how Benedict adapts the words of Psalm 34, it becomes clear that he understands fully the experience of baptism and monastic vocation as a humble recognition of the reality of God's goodness reaching out and calling to us. He begins with the words: "Come and listen to me, sons; I will teach you the fear of the Lord," adapting Psalm 34:11 by replacing "children" with "sons." God invites all of us to learn the fear of the Lord, i.e., to discover the awesome but wonderful reality of God's loving presence in our world.

Benedict continues his adaptation of Psalm 34 by expressing God's call in terms of a search for generous hearts: "Seeking his workman in a multitude of people, the Lord calls out to him and lifts his voice again: 'Is there anyone here who yearns for life and desires to see good days?' (v. 12)" (Prol 14-15). The divine call is a present reality because it never ceases. Whether it is heard depends upon the readiness of humans to ask for help or the readiness of monastics to deal with the sense of emptiness that caused them to seek out the monastery.

Benedict continues: "If you hear this and your answer is 'I do,' God then directs these words to you: If you desire true and eternal life, 'keep your tongue free from vicious talk and your lips from all deceit; turn away from evil and do good; let peace be your quest and aim' (Psalm 34:13-14)" (Prol 16-17). Both the Christian neophyte, and the monastic, who intensifies that baptismal commitment, must be converted to a radical kind of honesty that avoids selfish and defensive behavior and practices the kind of love that promotes the ideal of *shalom*, or blessed existence for all.

Finally, Benedict recalls the promise of Psalm 34: "Once you have done this, 'my eyes will be upon you and my ears will listen for your prayers' (v. 15)" (Prol 18). God's call is not, therefore, a whimsical gesture; it persists and represents a constant attentiveness, for God's eyes are never shut and his ears are never closed. This is only one of many examples of Benedict's acute awareness of the presence of God, in the lives of the baptized as well as in the sacred space of the monastery.

Therefore, just as the baptismal words expressed God's affirmation of the human Jesus in preparation for his ministry, so also does Jesus extend that same loving invitation to all of us. Benedict shows how well he understood this when he reminds his followers that they must fully exploit the implications of this loving invitation. "In his goodness, (God) has already counted us as his sons, and therefore we should never grieve him by our evil actions. With his good gifts which are in us, we must obey him at all times that he may never become the angry father who disinherits his sons..." (Prol 5-6). The loving call of God is, therefore, a standing invitation. And the inheritance that this loving Father holds for us is nothing less than the joys of heaven, for "'he has called us to his kingdom' (1 Thes 2:12)" (Prol 21). Our only concern must be that we do not reject or ignore this gracious call.

THE EXAMPLE OF ABRAHAM

When Benedict emphasizes the personal nature of God's call, he is perfectly in harmony with the classic vocations of Israel's holy ones. Notable among such vocations was that of Abraham. He was an old man with no plans for travel or adventure when God burst into his life and commanded him to set out for parts unknown. There was no haggling or hesitation: "So Abram went, as the Lord had told him" (Gn 12:4).

With the call to Abraham came extravagant promises: "I will make of you a great nation..." (Gn 12:2). "(The Lord) brought (Abram) outside and said, 'Look toward heaven and number the stars, if you are able to count them.' Then (the Lord) said to him, 'So shall your descendants be'" (Gn 15:5). But there seemed to be no possible way to realize these promises since Abraham and Sarah were childless. Nonetheless, Abraham "grew strong in his faith as he gave glory to God" (Rom 4:20). His ability to trust God's promises did not come from the logic of God's message but rather from the bond of trust that grew ever stronger between him and the God who had called him to the journey of faith.

Benedict knows all about this journey of faith and how it will test the perseverance of the monastic disciple. But he also knows about the personal bond of trust that can develop between the monastic and the God who has spoken his or her name in love. Therefore, Benedict does not hesitate to offer God's splendid assurance to those who trust the divine call: "'my eyes will be upon you, and my ears will listen for your prayers, and even before you ask me, I will say to you, Here I am' (Is 58:9)" (Prol 18). This "here I am," spoken by God, greets the "here I am" of such models as Abraham (Gn 22:1) and Isaiah (6:8). It awaits the monastic disciple also when he or she hears the loving call of God: "Is there anyone here who yearns for life and desires to see good days?" (Ps 34:13), and gladly answers, "I do" (Prol 15-16).

JESUS CALLS HIS APOSTLES

When Jesus called the twelve, he "gave them authority over unclean spirits, to cast them out, and to cure every disease and every sickness" (Mt 10:1). He also warned them about opposition and suffering. However, the love that called them would also accompany and support them: "And even the hairs of your head have all been counted. So do not be afraid; you are of more value than many sparrows" (Mt 10:30-31).

In John's version of the call of the disciples, special significance is attached to the call of Peter, Philip and Nathanael. When Jesus first met Peter, he said to him: "You are Simon son of John. You are to be called Cephas" (Jn 1:42). The name is immediately interpreted as "Peter" and "Rock." The first requirement in disciples is, therefore, that they be able to make a firm and reliable commitment. When Philip told Nathanael that he had found the messiah, he responded: "Can anything good come out of Nazareth?" (Jn 1:46). Philip then illustrated another quality for discipleship, for he responded simply: "Come and see" (Jn 1:46), thereby showing that he was open to the unexpected and not blinded by provincial prejudice. Finally, Nathanael himself illustrated a quality of discipleship when Jesus said of him: "Here is truly an Israelite in whom there is no deceit" (Jn 1:47). For God's call can only be heard by those who are personally truthful and genuine. Anyone who is acquainted with the Rule of Benedict will recognize immediately the importance of these qualities in the monk who responds to God's call, for he must certainly be firm in his professed intention and open to the unexpected demands of obedience and without falsehood in his stance of humility.

"IF TODAY YOU HEAR GOD'S VOICE" (Ps 95:8)

Benedict's awareness of the primacy of God's call in the process of salvation accounts no doubt for his special emphasis on the words of Psalm 95 which he asked his monks to say every day at the beginning of Vigils (RB 9:3). This psalm begins with a joyous recognition of God's goodness: "O come, let us sing to the Lord; let us make a joyful noise to the rock of our salvation" (v. 1). Such goodness is cause for worship: "O come, let us worship and bow down, let us kneel before the Lord, our Maker" (v. 6). Then comes the plea that caught the eye of Benedict as he writes in the Prologue: "Let us open our eyes to the deifying light and with thunderstruck ears let us hear the voice from heaven that every day calls out this charge: 'If today you hear his voice, harden not your hearts' (Ps 95:8)" (Prol 9-10) (my translation).

We should note how Benedict insists that this call of God, expressed in terms of a biblical theophany, is heard *every day* and has about it an urgency that demands instant attention. There are, it seems, fairly obvious resonances between this text, as Benedict interprets it, and the baptismal voice from heaven that addressed Jesus. Jesus "softened" his heart to receive this voice and made himself vulnerable in the love that would flow from that freedom. Every Christian, and especially the monastic person, is challenged by Benedict to imitate as much as possible this generosity of Jesus.

A LOVING FATHER

We will say more about the response to God's call in the next chapter. However, the call and the response are so intertwined that it is almost impossible to separate them completely. And so we note that Benedict's awareness of the persistent and ever-present call of God demands that the monastic be constantly intent on *listening*. That is the first word of the Rule and it echoes to the very end. "Listen carefully, my son, to the master's instructions, and attend to them with the ear of your heart" (Prol 1).

The words of the master are to be heeded, not just because the master is a wise man, but primarily because he is a medium by which God's call is made present. The divine call is thus extended through human agents. Benedict leaves no doubt about this when he speaks of the abbot's responsibility to align his message with the one from God. "Therefore, the abbot must never teach or decree or command anything that would deviate from the Lord's instructions" (RB 2:4).

Moreover, just as in the case of Jesus' baptism, this voice of the spiritual master who invites all to consider the monastic way of life is the voice of a father. "This is advice from a father who loves us; welcome it and faithfully put it into practice" (Prol 1). And then, a few verses later, we read: "In his goodness, God has already counted us as his sons..." (Prol 5). Just as the loving call of God became incarnate in Jesus, the Word of God, so it is interpreted and focused by the loving invitation of the abbot as spiritual master.

The loving call of God is present therefore everywhere and at all times. It is addressed to all human beings, and not just to monastics. It is a call to leave the darkness and the chaos so as to be a new creature, loved and loving. Part of the chaos that continues to struggle against creation is the noise of a world where almost everything is called important except what is really important. This call is received in faith, and the response may vary greatly according to individual gifts, but it will always be a response that converts freedom into loving service. The response of the monastic tends to be more radical than most, but it remains essentially the same response that is expected of every believer.

3

A Journey of Faith

*"...let us set out on this journey with the Gospel
for our guide..."* (Prol 21).

God's gracious and insistent call awaits a human
response. This response may take many forms but it will
always result in a journey of conversion. Since conversion
is always a difficult and painful process, the journey will
not be made unless there is strong and persistent motivation. Such motivation will come primarily from a vision of
faith that draws one toward the future and enables one to
let go of the past. However, long before such a vision can be
operative, there must be a solid grounding in the acknowledgement of personal need.

NO TRUE RESPONSE WITHOUT HUMILITY

Nothing can happen in the process of salvation without
humility. As a spiritual master, Benedict certainly understood this, and this accounts no doubt for the careful attention he pays to humility in Chapter 7 of the Rule. We must
be careful to note that Benedict's understanding of humility
has almost nothing in common with its meaning in our
modern culture. Although it may indeed manifest itself in a
manner that is self-deprecating, it does not do so out of a
sense of low self-esteem. Rather, it is a simple recognition of

the reality of one's limitations, especially in relation to God. To be humble is to be realistic about what one can or cannot achieve by personal effort. It is opposed, not to self-esteem, but to the illusion of personal autonomy.

This concept of humility is clearly represented in the scriptures. When we consider that decisive moment in Israel's history which is the exodus, we note that the process of divine intervention and deliverance could begin only after the Hebrew slaves cried out for help: "...the Israelites groaned under their slavery, and they cried out. Out of the slavery their cry for help rose up to God" (Ex 2:23). There is no indication in the text that they cried out to Yahweh, whom they probably did not know. It simply states that they cried out for help, with the clear implication that they recognized their inability to deal with their predicament without the assistance of someone who could challenge the pharaoh.

This may seem to be a fairly simple matter of recognizing that humans are not God. However, a real and honest acknowledgement of need is by no means a simple matter. Any therapist who has dealt with cases of addiction can testify to this. The problem is that our culture esteems control and autonomy so highly that we find it embarrassing to acknowledge any really significant need. Moreover, when we do recognize needs, we usually do so only on condition that help comes in an acceptable form. Unconditional honesty is always very difficult. By contrast, a truly honest and humble cry for help will always accept without complaint whatever remedies the helper may decide are needed. There is little chance for real healing where trust in the therapist is lacking.

We see a classic example of how essential humility is for personal conversion in the exchange between Jesus and the Pharisees in chapter nine of John's gospel. Jesus cures a blind man and, by declaring that this identifies him as the "light of the world," demands a decision for or against himself by all who see what has happened. "Jesus said, 'It is for judgment that I have come into this world—to give sight to the sightless and to make blind those who see.' Some Pharisees who were present asked, 'Do you mean that we are blind?' 'If you were blind,' said Jesus, 'you would not be guilty, but because you claim to see, your guilt remains'" (9:39-41). The Pharisees would have been happy to accept Jesus on their own terms but, since he demanded that they abandon all their vested interests, they chose to reject his light, claiming that they already had a light with which to see. Real humility, because it is real honesty, is always costly.

HUMILITY MEANS ACCEPTING REALITY

Benedict certainly shared this biblical view of humility. When he writes that "The first degree of humility is, then, that a man keep the fear of God always before his eyes" (RB 7:10), he taps into a rich biblical theme, particularly in the wisdom tradition. There, the fear of God did not mean a cringing before God's majesty resulting in a kind of paralysis. Rather, it emphasized the reality of a human creature's relationship with his or her creator. It did not deny the human creature's rights and responsibilities but simply recognized that they must be harmonized with the superior rights of God. The opposite of such fear of God would be a prideful and illusory claim to complete autonomy. This is so fundamental that it is reflected in the story of the first sin. For Adam and Eve are said to have sinned by eating of the tree which symbolized the limitation on their freedom under God. To fear the Lord, therefore, means simply to let God be God or, in other terms, to accept reality.

Benedict expresses this view again in his unusual interpretation of a passage from Psalm 131: "If I had not a humble spirit, but were exalted instead, then you would treat me like a weaned child on its mother's lap" (v. 2)

(RB 7:4). In the original context, this weaned child seems to be a model of confidence as it senses the protective presence of its mother. Benedict, however, sees the weaned child as one who feels rejected because its mother has decided that it must now give up a privilege of infancy. In a similar manner, the humble monastic will accept the assertion of divine sovereignty even though that means giving up something once precious but now incompatible with expected growth. This is humility because it is reality.

There are, of course, many levels of reality. An outer layer is a succession of more or less ephemeral experiences of good or evil. God's gracious call may very well be recognized in these superficial manifestations of goodness. For God speaks in many voices. However, such experiences have no depth to them and are easily cancelled by similar experiences of evil. We must not despise such superficial blessings; sunshine on one's picnic or recess for a school child is an occasion for joy and gratitude. Nonetheless, it is a deeper and more mysterious kind of goodness that truly conveys God's loving call, and such goodness is experienced only through the gift of faith. The reality of our weakness and sinfulness is evident everywhere; the reality of God's goodness is usually deeper and more mysterious.

FAITH ENABLES US TO TRUST REALITY

The mysterious but powerful gift of faith takes us on a journey into an ever deeper appreciation of God's presence and goodness in the hidden recesses of life. Benedict captures the sense of this when he describes the dynamics of the monastic journey of conversion. "With loins girded by faith and the observance of good works, let us set out on this journey, with the Gospel for our guide, that we may deserve to see him who has called us to his kingdom" (Prol 21) (my translation). God's loving call invites us to make this journey by which we grow toward the kingdom. And it is faith that provides the motivation which will make that journey a wonderful opportunity rather than a burdensome necessity.

Benedict's understanding of faith was drawn from the scriptures, and when we consider the many places where scripture, speaks about faith we note that two texts in particular are helpful in discovering this biblical perspective. The first of these is found in chapter three of St. Paul's letter to the Romans. Paul has spent the previous two and a half chapters surveying the sad condition of sinfulness among both Gentiles and Jews, so that he must conclude: "...we have already charged that all, both Jews and Greeks, are under the power of sin" (3:9).

Now, however, the goodness of God manifested in Jesus Christ has made it possible for all without exception to escape the bondage of sin, a miracle that is achieved through the power of faith or, as Paul puts it, "...they are now justified by (God's) grace as a gift, through the redemption that is in Christ Jesus" (3:24). The words "grace as a gift" hardly do justice to the literal translation which reads, "after the manner of a gift, by his favor," which is an obvious redundance for the purpose of emphasis. The plain implication is that faith enables one to discover the gift of goodness that God has put in human life. This inexhaustible reservoir of divine goodness has been obscured by layers of sin and violence and injustice, but faith allows one to cut through those thick layers and to tap into that sea of goodness and to be liberated by the forgiveness and affirmation that are found there.

The revelation of this goodness comes through God's "redemption that is in Christ Jesus" because it is in Christ that this goodness has become incarnate. When we see his act of total self-giving for our sake, we can begin to understand in what sense God has said to all of us, through him, "You are my beloved children; I love you very much." It is in faith, therefore, that we discover endlessly the extent of that goodness just as it is in faith that we respond by opening our arms to that love and by allowing it to heal and strengthen us.

Another important biblical reference to the power of faith is found in Hebrews 11:1, where we read: "Now faith is the assurance of things hoped for, the conviction of things not seen." In this passage, faith is presented as such a solid foundation of trust in God's goodness that it makes hope possible. One stands on solid ground and sees the illuminated horizon gleaming with God's promise.

It is also an antidote to the kind of skepticism that will accept nothing that cannot be understood and thereby controlled. The "things not seen" are in fact the only really important things in life, such as love and happiness. We never really control these precious gifts. When we do try to control them, they are destroyed. Faith, however, gives us the courage to trust the gift that God has put in life and in the future, for the reality of God's goodness gradually becomes the only really trustworthy element in our lives.

From this perspective, faith is an awakening to a whole new vision of reality which discovers divine goodness in even the most unlikely places. This enables the believer to put aside a pessimistic, merely rational outlook that sees goodness as an occasional or sporadic occurrence in a world dominated by evil. Instead it makes possible a positive conviction about the victory of God's love and goodness, even though that victory may be obscured at times by a dramatic but relatively superficial appearance of evil.

MONASTIC FAITH EMBRACES MYSTERY

Benedict draws upon this biblical understanding of faith when he says that faith will enable the monastics to undertake resolutely that spiritual journey that will lead them to the final victory of divine goodness in the kingdom. Accordingly, when Benedict declares that the monastic must "gird his loins by faith" (Prol 21) (my translation), we may assume that he has in mind the description in Exodus of the manner in which the Passover meal is to be eaten: "This is how you shall eat it: your loins girded, your sandals on your feet, and your staff in your hand, and you shall eat it hurriedly" (12:11). This description is, of course, that of a person who is prepared for a journey. In the case of Israel, it is a question of their journey through the Sinai desert to the promised land, a journey which became the prototype of all journeys from bondage to freedom. For Benedict, the journey is a spiritual one that leads the monastic, and all other Christians, from the bondage of sin and fear through the desert of God's mystery to the promised land of heaven.

Israel's journey through the desert of Sinai took on symbolic implications already in the Hebrew scriptures, and this was further exploited in the Christian tradition. It is important to note that the Hebrew word that is usually translated "desert" actually means simply a place that is unexplored and unsurveyed. It means a "wilderness" in the original sense of that term, namely, a wild, undomesticated place. In Israel's case, it happened to be a desert, but it could just as well have been a jungle. This fact takes on special significance when we note that, in its symbolic meaning, the desert represents mystery. Moreover, since Israel enters this space at God's behest, it represents divine mystery.

Since the unknown is always a source of fear and anxiety, the Israelites were soon begging Moses to take them back to Egypt. For, even though Egypt represented bondage and oppression, it was at least a place that "made sense." It also represented the known and familiar past, as opposed to the unknown future. The fear of Israel was greatly intensified when Joshua led a scouting party into Canaan and they returned with frightening tales of a place occupied by giants whose cities seemed impregnable. "Then all the congregation raised a loud cry, and the people wept that night. And all the Israelites complained against Moses and Aaron; the whole congregation said to them, 'Would that we had died in the land of Egypt! Or would that we had died in this wilderness'" (Nm 14:1-3). The journey of faith does not, of course, remove the "giants" that lurk in our future, but it does allow us to neutralize their threat by our trust in God's goodness.

THE MONASTIC JOURNEY OF FAITH

Benedict's predilection for Psalm 95 is a clear indication that he understood the spiritual or symbolic significance of this journey through the wilderness. For it is precisely in this psalm that reference is made to Israel's failure to trust God when they were faced with the terrors of the unknown future: "Do not harden your hearts, as at Meribah, as on the day at Massah in the wilderness, when your ancestors tested me, and put me to the proof, though they had seen my work" (vv. 8-9). We see then that the only way to deal with this terrifying, unknown future is to convert one's past experience of goodness into trust in the one who was the source of that goodness.

Such biblical imagery provides the context for Benedict's celebrated summary of the monastic experience in the final verses of the Prologue: "Do not be daunted immediately by fear and run away from the road that leads to salvation. It is bound to be narrow at the outset. But as we progress in this way of life and in faith, we shall run on the path of God's commandments, our hearts overflowing with the inexpressible delight of love" (Prol 48-49). The narrow path represents an experience of anxiety as the road chosen leads one into the uncharted and threatening territory of true self-knowledge and the unmasking of illusions. It is hoped that an ever more vibrant faith will enable the monastic to find stronger evidence of God's goodness precisely in that reality that seemed at first so difficult to embrace.

Ideally, faith will rise to the challenge of this journey into the wilderness and will enable the believer to deal with that divine mystery which is usually experienced as a future that does not conform to one's plans. And to the extent that this happens the heart of the monastic will expand with the discovery of goodness in the deeper reality of God's plan. This unexpected discovery will cause him or her to begin to run eagerly toward that future which has now been converted by faith from threat into promise. It is precisely this kind of transformation that represents that victory of faith over the world of doubt and despair which is celebrated by the author of the first letter of John: "And this is the victory that conquers the world, our faith. Who is it that conquers the world but the one who believes that Jesus is the Son of God?"(5:4-5).

Although Benedict does not refer to the eucharist except in passing, we can assume that he realized that it was related to the Passover meal of ancient Israel. In that case, he may also have recognized the role of that sacred meal as a sacrifice offered to God to invoke divine protection during the dangerous journey that Israel was about to undertake. As such, both that meal and the eucharist represent a commitment to undertake a journey of conversion from a past that was understood to a future that was full of mystery. This is a necessary journey because the past which is left behind is doomed while the future, for all its apparent dangers, is the source of life. The true meaning of the eucharist is betrayed, therefore, when it is portrayed and defended as a comforting reminder of how things used to be rather than as a challenge to face the future and to change in accordance with the needs of that future. (For further discussion of this dimension of the eucharist, see my article in *Worship*: "Passover and Eucharist.") Far from being mere defenders of tradition, monastics should see themselves as pioneers that lead the way into a new and more promising future.

CHRISTIAN OBEDIENCE

If the journey of faith is a journey from bondage, through the wilderness of divine mystery, to ultimate freedom, it is a journey that cannot be made successfully without a guide. It is in this context that Benedict understood and appreciated the role of obedience. For him, obedience was not a device for assuring good order or even for guaranteeing the production of good works. Rather, he saw it as a commitment to seek and accept spiritual guidance about the best way to make the difficult journey through that untracked wilderness which represents the mystery of God's will in human lives. Monastics seek guidance from their superiors, but all Christians need such help and will find it in spiritual direction or the sacrament of reconciliation or from good and honest friends.

In any case, such guidance is indispensable if one hopes to discover the truth about one's talents and possibilities and if one expects to be able to use those gifts in a truly unselfish manner. In spite of good intentions and noble resolutions, selfishness has a way of insinuating itself into all human projects. How much more so when that project is the painful business of personal conversion. It is so much easier to live in the illusion of the importance of one's own projects than to have another evaluate them in terms of their usefulness for the benefit of all.

To submit oneself to an independent judgment on the unselfish nature of one's evaluation and deployment of personal gifts is an act of humility that is possible only where there is a strong desire to make that journey of faith and to accept whatever help is necessary to do so successfully. If one has no intention of making that spiritual journey, then there is, of course, no need of a guide. Accordingly, obedience will be an intolerable burden to those who have found their comfortable niche and have no interest in raising questions about whether they should stay there. On the other hand, where the journey is more important than one's own present project, one will want to consult a guide constantly about the best way to deal with tomorrow's challenge to live unselfishly.

MONASTIC OBEDIENCE

In the matter of specifically monastic obedience, Benedict has garnered the wisdom painfully discovered by the earliest monks of the Egyptian desert. They began with noble ideals but they soon learned how dangerous it was to make this journey of conversion alone. Their ascetical excesses and foolish competition soon convinced them of the need for guidance. It must surely be for this reason that Benedict makes the rather surprising statement that monks "desire to have an abbot over them" (RB 5:12). And, in chapter 71 of the Rule, he calls obedience a "blessing" (v. 1). Such positive evaluations of the difficult virtue of obedience can be made, of course, only by one who is so realistic and wise that he understands the grave danger of trying to make this journey without a guide.

Guidance on the journey of conversion comes primarily from the superior, but Benedict also asks his followers to seek guidance from each other: "Obedience is a blessing to be shown to all, not only to the abbot but also to one another as brothers, since we know that it is by this way of obedience that we go to God" (RB 71:1). For monastics who have lived in a world where obedience has almost always

been of the hierarchical or vertical variety, it is refreshing to
hear Benedict insist on an obedience that is communal and
horizontal. But this is perfectly consistent with the understanding of obedience which sees it as guidance rather than
dictate. Nothing could be more natural and wholesome
than to seek the advice of trusted friends or fellow community members about new initiatives that one may be con-
templating.

Ultimately, of course, the superior must be brought into
this discerning about what the unselfish use of gifts will
mean in one's life. The superior's role will be decisive but it
will first be a continuation of the process of dialogue about
what the Spirit wishes all of us to do. It may help to realize
that there is always a hidden third party present for such
discussions, namely, the people who are meant to benefit
from the proper use of our gifts. Obedience is not primarily
about whose will is stronger or whose authority is greater
but about how unselfish love can be made truly effective.

I had occasion to experience this dynamic of monastic
obedience when I went to my archabbot, Egbert Donovan,
O.S.B., to suggest that, after fifteen years as rector of our
seminary, it might be time to use my talents in some other
way. I noted that Pope Paul VI was elected the same year
that I was appointed rector and that, since he had just died,
it might be a sign from heaven that I should make a change
too. (A little humor is not out of place in these situations.)
The archabbot listened patiently and then said, quite simply: No, we need someone with experience in that position.
So I served as rector for two more years. I think that is an
apt example of how obedience is usually experienced in a
monastic setting.

Benedict was aware that the superior too must be obedient to the Spirit. Otherwise, he would never have written in
chapter three that the abbot must consult the whole community before making an important decision. In a very real

sense, he is telling the abbot that he too must be obedient to the Spirit who often speaks most clearly through the advice of the community members. For it is the Spirit who best understands the journey of faith and who is therefore the ultimate guide on that journey.

God's gracious call summons all to make the journey of faith. We can do so only to the extent that we are made real through humility and learn, through faith, to see the goodness in reality. This journey of conversion is difficult at times and cannot be accomplished without guidance. This is true for all believers; monastics only focus on it with greater intensity.

4

Christ, in Whom We Are Loved

"The love of Christ must come before all else" (RB 4:21).

The next two chapters will be concerned with that reality which is the very heart of Benedict's spirituality, namely, the presence of Christ as the one in whom monastics receive the liberating love of God and through whom they are able to share that love with others. Esther de Waal sums this up beautifully when she writes: "The way of Benedict is pervaded with the idea of sacramental encounter with Christ, in liturgy and office, in material things, in the circumstances of daily life, above all in people" (*Living with Contradiction: Reflections on the Rule of Benedict*, p. 39).

We have already noted that the baptismal story of Jesus is meant to show how Jesus was constantly affirmed by his heavenly Father and how he became the very incarnation of that call to all human beings. In and through Christ, the loving call of God resonates throughout creation, and for every person it has the same message: You are my beloved child; I love you very much. Those who are humble and realistic about their condition of bondage are ready to hear that call and to respond to it in faith. There is no other way to begin the journey of salvation.

MONASTICS SEEK GOD IN THE RADICAL FUTURE

The monastic person in every tradition, Christian or otherwise, hears the divine call in a very specific way. It is a summons that reveals, at one and the same time, the ultimate inadequacy of everything offered by this world and the need to seek and find the transcendent One. It is as though one had caught a glimpse of the One who transcends everything and can never be satisfied now with anything less than that. In a sense, it is like Isaiah who, in the vision that accompanied his vocation (Is 6), saw the fringes of the robe of Yahweh and knew instinctively that he must now spend the rest of his life searching for the vision of God's face.

From a biblical perspective, the temporal mode is primary. Accordingly, a monastic vocation for people formed by the bible will be a search for the transcendent One who is to be found, not high above this earth, but in the radical future. The end of time, or the *eschaton*, becomes that powerful magnetic force that pulls everything toward the end of history and makes all of human life an experience of Advent. God is truly present here but in an elusive way that always implies the ache of unfulfillment. We heirs of Greek and western culture must make a conscious effort to understand this temporal perspective. We like to make things stand still so that they can be subjected to scientific analysis.

The biblically formed person, however, is more interested in the direction in which something is moving. In a Hebrew sentence the verb precedes the noun; the active or dynamic element has priority over the static or defined reality. St. Paul is a witness to this biblical sense of reality when he writes to the Philippians: "...forgetting what lies behind and straining forward to what lies ahead, I press on toward the goal for the prize of the heavenly call of God and Christ Jesus" (3:13-14).

Since the Christian monastic vocation presupposes a biblical formation, it is therefore a decision to search for God in the radical future, the future that is beyond the remaining years of this life. This is the context in which Benedict prescribes that the one condition above all for determining the validity of a monastic candidate's vocation is that he or she be one who is consumed by this search for God: "The concern must be whether the novice truly seeks God" (RB 58:7). This has nothing to do with the novice's interest in theology; rather, it is about a deep desire to see the face of God after having glimpsed the fringes of God's robe. Moreover, it is about the future, not the past.

All biblically formed believers are, of course, committed to a search for God as one who calls to us from the ultimate future. In this sense, all believers participate in the monastic search for God. However, the vowed monastic quest is more radical and visible. It is, in fact, intended to be a splendid service to other Christians since it reminds them that they too must avoid being so immersed in the things of this world that they forget the reality and primacy for all Christians of this journey to God. Both monastic and non-monastic Christians would fully agree with the author of Hebrews that "here we have no lasting city, but we seek the city which is to come" (Heb 13:14). However, monastic Christians exemplify this in a more dramatic way and thereby become witnesses to its importance for the whole church.

CHRIST IS THE WAY

It is well known that monasticism flourishes in non-Christian traditions also. This is most obvious among the Buddhists. What these monks share with Christian monastics is their common quest for a meaning in life that is ultimately beyond this world. They differ from Christian monastics, of course, in the fact that they do not know

Christ as the one in whom that search is made. By contrast, Christ is at the very center of the quest for Christian monastics. (Of course, it is quite possible that the non-Christian may live this commitment in a Christ-like way without being conscious of that fact, while a Christian monastic may fill his or her life with the name of Christ without ever entering deeply into the reality of what Christ means.)

Christ is at the center of the Christian monastic vocation, first of all, because he has already made that journey, but also, and primarily, because he is the one in whom that journey can be made in the quickest and surest way. Benedict reflects this conviction when he tells his followers that "The love of Christ must come before all else" (RB 4:21). This can only mean that all other realities in the life of monastics must be subordinate to their passionate and personal attachment to Christ.

The central role of Christ in the monastic journey reflects the New Testament insistence that he is the "way." The clearest example of this is found in John 14:5-6. "Thomas said to him, 'Lord, we do not know where you are going. How can we know the way?' Jesus said to him, 'I am the way, and the truth, and the life. No one comes to the Father except through me.'" As Raymond Brown has pointed out, "the way, and the truth and the life" are not to be understood here as three separate realities identified with Jesus. Rather, these realities are interconnected in the sense that Christ is the way *because* he teaches the truth and this *leads* to true life (*The Gospel of John*, II, 630). Accordingly, we must hear and embrace Christ's wisdom if we wish to be united with him in true and lasting life. At the center of this wisdom is the challenge to live unselfishly. This is the only way to the Father, and it is the Father who is for monastics, as for all Christians, that transcendent One who is the object of their lifelong quest.

CHRIST REVEALS THE FATHER'S LOVE

If Christ is the only way because he teaches the truth, the very first element in that truth is the revelation of the hidden Father's love of all human beings. Israel had always been conscious of the transcendent and hidden nature of God. Even Moses, whom God treated like a friend (Ex 33:20), was not allowed to see the divine face. Jesus came to reveal the deepest secrets of this hidden God. This is clearly stated in the last verse of the prologue of John's gospel: "No one has ever seen God. It is God, the only Son, who is close to the Father's heart, who has made him known" (1:18). The Greek verb used here means literally that Jesus has "interpreted" the Father for us.

And what we learn from this exposition or interpretation is that the transcendent and hidden God loves us more than we can ever understand. Jesus is himself the sign and proof of that love, not simply because he told us about it, but because he exemplified it in the most radical way. In fact, "God so loved the world that he gave his only Son, so that everyone who believes in him may not perish but may have eternal life" (Jn 3:16). Those who have faith in Christ, therefore, are those who know how to "read" the sign and to be convinced by it and to be liberated by this conviction. This is John's way of saying what the other gospels say when they record that God at the baptism called Jesus his beloved Son. And, as I have noted, this means that God has called all of us, in him, beloved children. Not only has God endowed Jesus with his infinite love, but he loves all of us in Jesus. Jesus, properly understood, means simply: God loves you.

NO FOLLOWING CHRIST WITHOUT FREEDOM

Biblical revelation reminds us constantly of something that is too often overlooked. We tend to be very clear and forceful about the responsibilities of Christians but we are not nearly so insistent on the importance of acquiring the freedom with which to meet those responsibilities. Successful Christian living does not mean to be responsible in some slavish or fearful way; it means to act responsibly out of freedom and with the kind of love that can exist only where there is true freedom.

This fact was brought home to me personally when I recalled having memorized the ten commandments as a child *without* the indispensable preamble, which reads: "I am the Lord your God who brought you out of the land of Egypt, out of the house of slavery" (Ex 20:2). This preamble is indispensable because it clearly shows that the commandments which follow are intended *only* for people who have already been liberated from bondage. Having acquired freedom and confidence, they are now prepared to use that newfound freedom in accordance with the wishes of the God whose love has made them free. Thus, their response will be an expression of gratitude as well as of obedience. Conversely, if these commandments are received by people who are not free, they will simply serve to increase their slavery, as guilt is added to the bondage they already experience. Of course, no one is absolutely free, but some degree of freedom is essential for a response of love.

As a wise spiritual master, Benedict certainly understood the importance of this experience of God's love as a precondition for the expression of that love in service to others. We find this conviction expressed in the Rule in those places where Benedict reminds all monastics that they are children of a loving divine Father. Thus, for example, he writes in the Prologue: "In his goodness, (God) has already counted us as his sons..." (v. 5). Later, after noting that the superior in some sense holds the place of Christ in the monastery, he applies a text of St. Paul to monastics: "You have received the spirit of adoption as sons by which we exclaim, 'Abba,

Father'" (Rom 8:15) (RB 2:3). Through Christ then (and the superior), the monastic is put in touch with the ineffable parental love of God.

TO BE IN CHRIST IS TO SHARE HIS
RELATIONSHIP WITH GOD

When Benedict appeals to Romans 8:15 to show that monastics have special access to the fatherly love of God, he reveals how well aware he was of Paul's conviction that the Christian not only knows the Father's love through Jesus but also that it is precisely this experience of God's love that makes the Christian believer one with Christ. This unity with Christ is most commonly expressed by Paul in his well-known insistence that every Christian exists in some way "in Christ" (e.g., Rom 6:2 and 8:1). It is important to note that this unity with Christ is not achieved by simply looking at Christ and trying to imitate him. Such a viewpoint is sometimes expressed in the question: What would Jesus do in this situation? Since it is almost impossible to picture Jesus in our time and culture, the answer is likely to be that he would do exactly what I wish to do. Such is definitely not the path to real conversion.

St. Paul would insist that we are in Christ and that we become like Christ *exactly to the extent that we experience God as Christ himself experienced him, that is, as loving, affirming and liberating Father.* It is, therefore, by knowing the Father and by experiencing the Father's love that we become one with Christ. And it is for this reason that all the eucharistic prayers, and most other prayers as well, are addressed to God the Father through Christ and in their common Spirit. Accordingly, the more we experience the reality of God as loving Father, the more we are united with the Son and the more we become like Christ and live "in Christ."

Carolyn Osiek has noted that this is reflected in the way

in which Paul understood the nature of Christian prayer. She writes: "I do not think that Paul (in prayer) was turned toward Christ, but toward God…he saw himself embedded as a dyadic personality *in* Christ, the root and ground of the common identity of Christians. Thus his famous phrase 'in Christ' is not a metaphor but a perception of reality" ("Paul's Prayer" in *Scripture and Prayer*, p. 149).

Moreover, to experience truly the Father's love is to be able, in Christ, to love those whom one could never love by one's own ability. Benedict shows how well he understood this when he lists among the Tools for Good Works: "Pray for your enemies out of love for Christ" (RB 4:72). This love "for Christ" is not a love that we in our poverty choose to offer; rather, it is the power to love divinely because we have, with Christ, discovered the love of the Father. This is that wonderful gift that makes us one with Christ and enables us to love as Christ loves.

For Benedict, everything is centered in this loving of Christ that has become our own loving and which establishes our identity as true Christians. He writes: "Your way of acting must be different from the world's way; the love of Christ must come before all else" (4:20-21). In other words, it is precisely in the way that Christ's loving has become the center of our being that we are distinguished from the world, from all those who have not known or accepted Christ in faith. Ultimately, it is the Father's love that finds expression in Christ and in all those who have come to know and appropriate that love because they are one with Christ.

OBEDIENCE FOR LOVE'S SAKE

Such a participation in the loving of Christ enables monastics to embrace gracefully all the hardships that obedience may present for them. Since they have begun to participate in the liberating love of the Father, they have become so rich in that goodness that they can with relative ease let go of the need or comfort of doing things in their own way. Giving up their own wills has become possible and even joyful because they have found, in Christ, something that is infinitely more comforting. It is always easier to deal with some hardship after receiving good news. And the best news that one could ever receive is the experience of the gospel reality of God's special love for us in Christ. Complete autonomy, even if it were possible, ceases to be an ideal.

When monastics are truly humble, they live in the reality *both* of their own need *and* of God's love for them. Small wonder, then, that Benedict can write that "The first degree of humility is unhesitating obedience, which comes naturally to those who cherish Christ above all" (lit. "hold nothing whatever dearer to themselves than Christ") (RB 5:1-2). Prompt and generous obedience is possible for monastics, therefore, not because their will power has developed, but because they have begun to experience the love of God which liberates them for generosity. The more literal translation makes it quite clear that this spontaneous goodness does not come from simply looking at Christ with love but rather it happens because there is nothing in life that monastics consider more important or more precious than the presence of Christ. Christ has quite simply become the center of their existence; they have begun to live in, and love with, Christ.

This deeply personal and passionate attachment to Christ is the heart of that "good zeal" which Benedict extols in chapter 72 of the Rule: "Just as there is a wicked zeal of bitterness which separates from God and leads to hell, so there is a good zeal which separates from evil and leads to God and everlasting life (RB 72:1-2). It is this experience of being exceedingly blest by the love of God in Christ that enables the monastic then to be patient with fellow community members beyond what would normally be possible. Indeed, one who is rich in God's love can afford to be poor in every other respect.

DEALING WITH TEMPTATIONS

Benedict also sees in this attachment to Christ the perfect and only truly effective antidote against the temptations that will assail monastics on their journey of conversion. Among the characteristics of the one who deserves to dwell in the Lord's tent, Benedict lists prominently the ability to ward off the devil's assaults. "He has foiled the evil one, the devil, at every turn, flinging both him and his promptings far from the sight of his heart. While these temptations were still young, he caught hold of them and dashed them against Christ" (Prol 28). Using phrases borrowed from Psalms 15 and 137, Benedict thus makes Christ the one in whom monastics will be safe from even the fiercest assaults of Satan.

This is an eminently wise observation. For anyone who has dealt with temptations to sin will recognize that these enticements are not effectively neutralized unless one can call to consciousness an alternative that is even more attractive. We have all observed that when a small child refuses to share its toy with a visiting cousin, the wise mother will not take the toy from the child forcibly but will simply find another toy that is even bigger and brighter. This will usually cause that child to relinquish cheerfully the toy that had previously seemed indispensable to its happiness.

This fact of common human experience also manifests the important difference between remorse and repentance. Remorse is that unpleasant experience that comes after the sin has been committed. It can be very intense but it rarely lasts long. That is why fire and brimstone sermons seldom lead to lasting conversion. By contrast, a sermon that enables us to recover our awareness of God's presence and goodness will lay the foundation for true repentance. For repentance not only regrets sin but also turns toward God whose goodness is now seen to be far more desirable than the apparent goodness of one's sin. Ultimately, it is only love that conquers sin. Benedict sees this divine goodness centered in the experience of Christ's presence so that, when that presence is evoked, it will be an effective antidote against all contrary attractions.

THE MEANING OF CELIBACY

It is also in this context of the monastics' passionate attachment to Christ that we can fully appreciate their dedication to the celibate ideal. Long before celibacy means the renunciation of marriage, it represents an exclusive and single-minded dedication to Christ as the center of one's existence. Celibacy may be chosen for other reasons, such as the fear of intimacy or, more positively, the desire to be free for one's chosen work. However, it is not authentic monastic celibacy if it is not centered ultimately in one's passionate attachment to Christ, for, in Benedict's words, the monk "holds nothing whatever more precious" than Christ (RB 5:2) (my translation). The same commitment to Christ is expressed also in chapter 72: "Let them prefer nothing whatever to Christ" (v. 11).

Of course, all Christians are invited to be passionately devoted to Christ, and many of them are no doubt better at this than some celibates. However, the celibate's commitment is in a context that makes this a primary witness because it is a professed, public and exclusive attention to Christ. Hopefully, the intensity of the commitment will be evident in both situations but the expression of it will be different. We no longer consider one way more perfect than the other because the difference lies more in the grace offered than in the response to it. Moreover, the generous celibate and non-celibate will no doubt sing happily together in the heavenly choir.

The single-minded commitment required in the celibate state is at issue also in Benedict's use of military imagery in the Rule. At the time of Benedict, military service was a lifelong commitment with a very strong element of personal loyalty. Some soldiers were even branded to express the irreversibility of their commitment, and this example was used by the fathers to illustrate the effect of the special character or mark conveyed in baptism. Already in verse three of the Prologue, Benedict suggests a parallel between monastic life and military service: "This message of mine is for you, then, if you are ready to give up your own will, once and for all, and armed with the strong and noble weapons of obedience to do battle for the true King, Christ the Lord" (v. 3). We should note that this commitment is decisive and final, for it is made "once and for all." The "weapons of obedience" would then be that readiness to subordinate one's own will and plans to the loving design of God expressed in Christ and made concrete in the superior's decisions.

The same sense of devoted and permanent commitment is conveyed in other texts where Benedict associates monastic life with that of military service. For example, he writes in chapter one that cenobites "serve (lit. do military service) under a rule and an abbot" (v. 2). Later on, he writes: "...wherever we may be, we are in the service of the same Lord and doing battle for the same King" (RB 61:10).

It is in the context of this pledged loyalty, no doubt, that we can best understand Benedict's strong language about the bonds that tie monastics to their community. After detailing carefully the preparation of a novice for profession, he concludes that the professed monastic "must be well aware that, as the law of the rule establishes, from this day he is no longer free to leave the monastery, nor to shake from his neck the yoke of the rule which, in the course of so prolonged a period of reflection, he was free either to reject or to accept" (RB 58:15-16). Later in the same chapter, Benedict acknowledges the possibility that a monastic might "agree to the devil's suggestion and leave the monastery" (v. 28). It is clear that he sees this, not as an optional career change, but as a real personal reneging on a freely pledged loyalty to Christ and the community.

Such a severe judgment can be made, of course, only where the formation of the young monastic has been truly effective and, more importantly, where that person has truly come to know the goodness of God revealed in Christ. A great many factors will contribute to this awakening of one's faith conviction about God's goodness. Notable among these are the loving affirmation of one's superior and community, and the precious support of family and friends, as well as daily reminders of divine love and care expressed in the psalms and other biblical readings.

In fact, Benedict wants the whole monastery to act in concert to help all the community members to come to an ever deeper awareness of the goodness of God made incarnate in Christ. This becomes the primary responsibility of the abbot, and it is for this reason that Benedict makes that bold statement that the abbot "is believed to hold the place of Christ in the monastery..." (RB 2:2). We will discuss this more thoroughly in Chapter 7, but it is necessary to mention it here in view of the superior's critical role in making the reality of Christ's love a vital element in the experience of the community. All of the other monastic officials share in this responsibility. Indeed, it is the primary duty of all the monks without exception. Absolutely nothing is of greater urgency than this experience of the presence of Christ in the community as the one who truly reveals the Father's infinite goodness.

BENEDICT'S EMPHASIS ON THE DIVINITY OF CHRIST

We know, of course, that when we speak of Christ we may be stressing either his divine or his human nature. There is no doubt that Benedict places the emphasis on Christ's divine nature. This is so true that, when he speaks of the abbot holding the place of Christ in the monastery, he does not hesitate to base this on that text from Paul in which Christians are said to cry out to God with the word "Abba" or "Father" (Rom 8:15; RB 2:3). It is clear that Paul meant God the Father in this text, but Benedict interprets the passage in a way that identifies Christ as Father. This is in keeping with monastic tradition (cf. *RB1980*, pp. 356-63) and reflects a tendency to affirm the loving, fatherly quali- ties in Christ as well as in God the Father.

Scholars have surmised that this was probably due to the rampant Arian heresy of Benedict's day, a heresy which denied the equality of Christ with the Father. It is probably for this reason also that Benedict never calls Christ "Jesus" and never refers to any events of the public ministry of Jesus except the passion. Another reason for this emphasis could be his conviction that Christ is such a perfect repre- sentation of the Father's goodness that, from our human perspective, the difference is difficult to notice. This view would be similar to that reflected in the passage in John's gospel where Jesus tells Philip: "Whoever has seen me has seen the Father" (14:9).

Christ is central to Benedict's spirituality, therefore, first of all as the one in whom we discover the goodness of the hidden God, who is revealed in him as loving Father. In the next chapter, we will consider the ways in which Christ is also the one in whom we are able to reach out to others in love and service. However, that generosity will always be possible only *to the extent* that we have been liberated and energized by the experience of God's love in Christ. Even our ability to sin pre-supposes that freedom, but, most of all, real freedom determines our ability to be a source of creative and liberating love in our world.

5

Christ, in Whom We Love Others

*"…so there is a good zeal which…leads to God
and everlasting life"* (RB 72:2).

Just as Christ is the one through whom the love of God is
fully revealed and in whom that love is experienced, so also
is he the one in whom that love becomes fruitful for the
benefit of others. The love of God cannot remain inactive.
Even before the beginning, that love reached out in the eternal Word and, through that Word, produced the blessings
of creation. Henceforth, anyone who participates in that
love and understands its nature will wish to reach out in
the same way and thus to become a blessing in the lives of
others.

Here again, the model is Christ. His baptismal experience
was a summarizing of all the love and affirmation of the
heavenly Father, both before and after that event. And, in
the freedom and strength received through that affirmation,
Jesus went forth to proclaim the advent of a new world
which would be transformed and animated by that divine
love. He illustrated the effects of this new creation by per-
forming deeds of kindness and mercy. When he cured the
lame and the blind and the deaf or drove out demons, he
was, in these latter days, once again overcoming the chaos
and darkness that preceded the first creation just as he was,
once again, liberating from the bondage of guilt and fear so

that all might be able to accept God's love and to offer it to others and thereby to enter into the kingdom.

A KINGDOM OF LOVE, NOT POWER

In Galilee, Jesus manifested power in service of love. However, the most perfect manifestation of God's love in Jesus came when he put aside his power and eloquence and accepted freely his destiny as one who would give his very life for others. In that moment of extreme vulnerability, Jesus showed that loving ultimately becomes trusting, for he trusted the Father's love in that dark mystery of passion and death. Thus, in both his strength and his weakness, Jesus allowed the love of God to flow through him and to change the world forever. In the process, of course, he made it his own love so that he has become and will remain forever the presence among us of God's powerful and transforming love.

All Christians have been and continue to be baptized in the reality of this divine love. In hearing the Father call them beloved children, they too are continuously empowered to perform works of kindness and mercy and liberation in their own Galilees. And they too will have the opportunity to express that loving in the difficult trusting that will be demanded by their own experience of weakness and loss of control in the process of aging and dying, for they too will have to make the journey to Jerusalem. Thus, the love of the hidden God which has been revealed in Jesus will hopefully flow through his followers also as they promote the kingdom and realize the new creation.

LOVING WITH CHRIST'S LOVE

This love of God translated into human idiom is not just human love that has been somehow blest. Rather, *it is a divine loving that transforms and energizes human loving, so that it is able to do what it could never do alone.* This special kind of loving is declared to be the distinctive characteristic of the true follower of Christ. "I will give you a new commandment, that you love one another. Just as I have loved you, you also should love one another. By this everyone will know that you are my disciples, if you have love for one another" (Jn 13:34-35).

These words of Jesus have often been understood to mean that Christians must simply imitate the loving of Jesus. It is far more likely, however, that the followers of Jesus are being asked to allow the love of Jesus to flow through them for the benefit of others. This is the interpretation of Raymond Brown who writes: "...love is more than a commandment; it is a gift, and like the other gifts of the Christian dispensation it comes from the Father through Jesus to those who believe in him. In 15:9, we hear, 'As the Father has loved me, so have I loved you'; and in both 13:34 and 15:12 the 'as I have loved you' emphasizes that Jesus is the source of the Christians' love for one another. (Only secondarily does it refer to Jesus as the standard of Christian love.)" (*The Gospel According to John* II, p. 612).

Therefore, just as Christians become one with Christ in receiving the Father's love, so also do they become one with Christ in making that love available to others. And it is this radically enhanced loving that becomes the distinguishing mark of all true followers of Christ. When we look more closely at this Christ-like kind of loving, we note that it derives more from the goodness of the one who loves than from the attractiveness of the one loved. By contrast, much human romantic loving seems to be based primarily on the attraction or beauty of the one who is loved. God's love, shared with us in Christ, does not despise such attraction, but it goes far beyond that. It participates in that characteristic of divine love which is clearly revealed already in the Hebrew scriptures.

For God did not love and liberate the Hebrew slaves because they were more beautiful or attractive than the Egyptians but simply because God is good and this kind of goodness reaches out instinctively to those who are most in need. Moreover, this kind of loving has almost miraculous power. For God's loving actually made the slaves beautiful, as well as free and resourceful. This kind of love is creative beyond imagination.

Finally, it was this experience of being freely loved that enabled Israel to discover the ultimate secret of human responsibility, namely, that true freedom must be used henceforth solely for loving others so that they also may be free. A classic expression of this responsibility that comes with being loved is found in Deuteronomy 24:17-18: "You shall not deprive a resident alien or an orphan of justice; you shall not take a widow's garment in pledge. Remember that you were slaves in Egypt and the Lord your God redeemed you from there; therefore I command you to do this." The Israelites are thus commanded to care for the most vulnerable among them because God loved and cared for them when they were vulnerable to oppression. The gift of love brings with it, therefore, the urgent responsibility to share that gift with others. Jesus models this for us, because he was loved into full freedom and then freely chose to give his life that we might be free. In this way, the love of God in Christ becomes our loving. Truly, then, it is Christ in whom we love others.

TRUE LOVE ALWAYS SEEKS TO LIBERATE

However, the strength received from being nourished by goodness must never become a source of pride or self-satisfaction. It is a strength that is given solely for the purpose of helping others who are still weak and frightened. Perhaps the only question that we will have to answer when it comes time to give an account of our lives will be: Did you let my people go? That is, did you use your gift of freedom to love others and thereby to help them to become free? Or, conversely, did you imitate the pharaoh by using your freedom to control and dominate and thus to keep others in their bondage of self-doubt and low self-esteem? Love that does not liberate in some way is not authentic love.

At first this kind of beneficent loving will be perhaps selective as it chooses where it thinks that loving is most needed. However, this tendency to be selective will gradually give way to an indiscriminate kind of loving which lets go of even that subtle control that is represented by choosing. I have often thought that this is the real point of that rather strange story in the gospel about a woman who survived seven husbands (Mt 22:23-28). When the Sadducees tested Jesus by asking whose wife she would be in heaven, he replied simply that they knew nothing about heaven, for, if they did, they would know that this will not be a problem there. I suspect that what Jesus was really saying was that the only people who merit heaven will be those who have moved beyond the kind of loving that is selective and will have become quite simply loving persons. In that case, no one will feel cheated because all alike will be warmed, equally and fully, by the environment of love created by such a person. Mother Teresa is a good example of this kind of loving. For it is hard to believe that anyone who meets her would ever feel cheated if she should spend a minute more with someone else.

This kind of loving appears to be exactly what Benedict has in mind when he speaks of the victory of loving over fear and competition in the life of the monastic. This is most evident in that beautiful passage in chapter seven, where he summarizes all the steps of humility in the following words: "Now, therefore, after ascending all these steps of humility, the monk will quickly arrive at that perfect love of God which casts out fear. Through this love, all that he once performed with dread, he will now begin to observe without effort, as though naturally, from habit, no longer out of fear of hell, but out of love for Christ, good habit and delight in virtue" (RB 7:67-69).

Benedict thus states that this victory of love in the life of monastics will be achieved "out of love of Christ, good habit and delight in virtue." Surely this can only mean that such monastics have begun to appropriate the loving of Christ and thus are becoming ever more united with him in his loving. Such a union with Christ in his loving is so consonant with the ideal that God wishes to see realized in his human creatures that it readily becomes a kind of connatural habit in that creature. Moreover, because it is so much in harmony with the true purpose of human behavior it will produce an experience of delight. Such joy is identical with that "inexpressible delight of love" to which Benedict refers at the end of the Prologue (v. 49).

LIBERATING LOVE CREATES COMMUNITY

This kind of loving concern will never seek to sacrifice individual characteristics in order to bring all members into conformity with some kind of ideal community person. Rather, it will strive to enable each member to discover and develop his or her distinctive personal gifts for the benefit of all. St. Paul taught this wisdom long ago and expressed it in chapter twelve of his first letter to the Corinthians: "To each is given the manifestation of the Spirit for the common good" (12:7). He goes on to describe how a body becomes sick when there is destructive competition among its members (1 Cor 12:14-25). Conversely, the body prospers when its members replace envy and resentment with sympathy and joy: "If one member suffers, all suffer together with it; if one member is honored, all rejoice together with it" (1 Cor 12:26).

This kind of harmonious mutual support does not come about because the members happen to have pleasant personalities. It is possible only where the love of Christ enables the members to value and cherish the interests of others without losing their own sense of identity and without sacrificing their distinctive personal qualities. The loving of Christ is thus made very personal and delightfully varied as it is refracted through the prism of a community of strong and distinctive personalities.

Such a minor miracle is made possible, according to Paul, through the presence in that community of the special kind of loving which is found in Christ and which he calls *agape*, that is, completely altruistic love. He describes its characteristics in 1 Corinthians 13:4-7. When one examines this important passage carefully, one is struck immediately by the lack of romantic features in this description of loving. Rather, the emphasis is on such prosaic qualities as patience, kindness, sensitivity, humility, tolerance, forgiveness and trust. These are the "everyday" virtues which create community far more effectively than either ephemeral attraction or those necessary but often tedious community meetings that try monastic patience. These humble virtues are in fact exactly what the love of Christ means when it begins to transform daily life. To love as a mere human being is wonderful, but to have that loving enhanced by blending it with the loving of Christ is to give it a power for good and for freedom that goes far beyond human possibilities.

THE CENOBITIC IDEAL

Benedict accepted the ancient ideal of the hermit as the most perfect exponent of monastic witness. But he also realized that most ordinary mortals could not successfully follow that route. Accordingly, he urged his followers to accept the support and encouragement provided by a life in community. Indeed, his Rule is written for "the strong kind, the cenobites" (RB 1:13). These are the ones "who belong to a monastery, where they serve under a rule and an abbot" (RB 1:2).

We have noted above that the kind of liberating love that is found in those who are united with Christ leads inevitably to the mutual concern and support that are characteristic of a truly Christian community. For Benedict, therefore, the monastic community is simply a more intense form of that life in Christ to which all Christians are called. And it follows that the dynamics of a monastic community are essentially the same as those of a community of believers who are not professed religious. Moreover, one of the principal services of monastics to their fellow Christians is this modeling of a truly functional community animated by the love of Christ.

This loving with the love of Christ is extolled by Benedict in chapter 72 of the Rule, a chapter that could justly be described as a Magna Carta for community living. For it is this kind of loving that constitutes the essence of that "good zeal which monks must foster with fervent love" (RB 72:3). Benedict is quick to point out the fruits that derive from such loving: "They should each try to be the first to show respect to the other, supporting with the greatest patience one another's weaknesses of body or behavior, and earnestly competing in obedience to one another" (RB 72:4-6).

Anyone who has lived long in a community will immediately recognize the implications of such a tolerant and forgiving attitude. There is nothing dramatic or spectacular about respecting and valuing another's views or about being tolerant and understanding in the face of another's annoying shortcomings, or about being sensitive to the wishes and needs of a confrere. However, it is precisely such attitudes that constitute the essence of successful community existence.

Benedict continues to describe, in chapter 72, further effects of such loving in union with Christ: "No one is to pursue what he judges better for himself, but instead, what he judges better for someone else" (RB 72:7). We note how St. Paul maintained that such an altruistic ideal is established on the example of Christ himself: "Do nothing from selfish ambition or conceit, but in humility regard others as better than yourselves" (Phil 2:3). Such an ideal challenges the Christian to take on that basic attitude which is at the heart of Christ's life and message: "Let the same mind be in you that was in Christ Jesus, who, though he was in the form of God, did not regard equality with God as something to be exploited, but emptied himself..." (Phil 2:5-7). It is only by loving "in Christ Jesus," therefore, that such an ideal is achievable by ordinary mortals.

In this same chapter 72, Benedict goes on to point out how this loving in and through Christ establishes the proper relationship between monastics themselves and all other persons in their lives: "To their fellow monks they show the pure love of brothers; to God, loving fear; to their abbot, unfeigned and humble love. Let them prefer nothing whatever to Christ, and may he bring us all together to everlasting life" (RB 72:9-11). Both love of the brothers or sisters and love of God must be genuine and respectful. The love of monastics for their superior must not, therefore, be tainted by political considerations, nor should it degenerate into presumptuous familiarity. And in all of these community relationships it will be a union of love with Christ that will establish the proper priorities, for it is in Christ alone that monastics can expect to reach that goal of everlasting life for which they entered the monastery in the first place.

When Benedict asks his followers to prefer nothing whatever to Christ, he is not simply saying that Christ should be the object of their love but he is also saying that their own loving must become in some sense the very loving of Christ. Then we can fully appreciate the way in which that abundance of love will overflow our own concerns and reach out to all who are needy. We will discuss this generosity more fully later in Chapter 7. Suffice it to mention here in summary fashion Benedict's deep concern for all who are in need: the sick, the old and the very young, travelers, and even delinquent monks. Indeed, this extraordinary compassion for human weakness sets Benedict apart from all his monastic predecessors in a way that can only be characterized as revolutionary.

Such exceptional sensitivity cannot be explained as the consequence of one's good nature. It is credible only as the kind of loving that is possible in human beings who have begun to love with the love of Christ himself. Benedict surely had this in mind when he lists among the Tools for Good Works: "Your way of acting must be different from the world's way; the love of Christ must come before all else" (RB 4:20-21). Or, again, "Pray for your enemies out of love for Christ" (RB 4:72).

THE CELIBATE'S RADICAL LOVING

We have already mentioned monastic celibacy and described it as a passionate and single-minded attachment to Christ. In the present context, where the fruitfulness of loving in Christ is at issue, celibacy takes on a special significance which is as difficult to explain as it is easy to experience. Since it represents an exclusive attachment to Christ, it causes celibates to be people who in a sense belong to everyone, as Christ has chosen to be equally the friend of all. Celibates are "unattached ones" because they are attached exclusively to Christ.

One must appeal to imagery to express the nature of this

special situation. Both Christ and the Christian have been compared at times to the classic fool or clown who is so out of harmony with the local order because he or she represents a wisdom from the transcendent world. This is a lonely and frequently misunderstood witnessing but it may also be the salvation of those who make room for it. The celibate would be the explicit representative of Christ as fool in the sense that Christ's teaching is called folly by St. Paul: "For the message about the cross is foolishness to those who are perishing..." (1 Cor 1:18). Such a "foolish one" raises questions that people would rather not think about but which are critically important for their ultimate happiness.

The portrayal of the celibate as fool for Christ is indirectly but dramatically expressed by Charles Williams in his book *The Greater Trumps*. This is the story of an ambitious family whose members are captivated by the possibility of controlling the destiny of the world through access to a golden table where the figures of the Tarot cards are endlessly dancing. In the same family there is a maiden aunt named Sybil who does not share their passion for power but seems quite content to be present and helpful in all kinds of simple ways. Thus, when they are fretting about whether their picnic will be fun, she is quietly making sandwiches. No one seems to know or care much about what may constitute happiness for her. More surprisingly, she does not appear to be concerned about this either.

Finally, after much maneuvering, the long-awaited day arrives when the family is actually in the presence of the golden table. They notice immediately that all the figures are moving rapidly with the remarkable exception of the Fool or Joker who is stationary in the center of the table. Finally, when they notice that Sybil is not there, they call her in to observe this strange phenomenon. But when she approaches the table, she sees the fool-figure in an altogether different way. As Williams tells it: "She surveyed the table carefully. 'Yes,' she said at last, 'there—no, there—no—it's moving so quickly I can hardly see it, dancing with the rest; it seems as if it were always arranging itself in some place which was empty for it'" (p. 74).

Sybil, whose very name suggests that she, as prophetess, possesses some secret wisdom, has adopted the way of Jesus, who lived out the folly of the cross in unselfish sacrifice. For that reason, she is the only one present who can understand the true role of the Christian who finds happiness simply by the seemingly foolish way of filling with love the empty spaces of need that are forever appearing among us. However, this is possible only when we are so joyfully committed to a deep personal love of Christ that it can be said that we love with Christ's love. For such persons, concern for personal happiness is no longer primary and may even seem almost irrelevant.

Williams himself seems to have sensed the connection between Sybil and the celibate state, for he has her nephew Henry say to her: "You're the marvel of virginity that rides in the Zodiac" (p. 54). In any case, authentic monastic celibates will certainly be those who know how to love passionately. For that reason they, like Sybil, will choose to fill up with their love and concern the empty places of need and distress which are never lacking in our world. As such, they will be channels for the indiscriminate loving of Christ. In other words, they will understand perfectly why Benedict would say: "The love of Christ must come before all else" (RB 4:21).

6

Trust

"Place your hope in God alone" (RB 4:41).

Trust is a beautiful virtue but, like most beautiful things, it is very fragile. It is the first casualty of violence and hatred. Nonetheless it is also indispensable to human happiness. In fact, there is a strong bond between love and trust and hope. For there can be no trust where love has not been experienced, and there is no real hope without trust.

There is, of course, an instinctive trusting which we see in very young children. However, that trust can easily be replaced by fear and suspicion when it is not nurtured by a loving parent or friend. Being loved by another becomes, therefore, an indispensable condition for both retaining and enhancing one's ability to trust. At the same time, the experience of betrayal teaches one to be cautious about trusting or even to stop trusting altogether. It seems, indeed, that trusting, like loving, is a perilous undertaking.

TRUST IN GOD TURNS THREAT INTO PROMISE

Though there seems to be peril in the trust given to individuals in one's everyday experience, that danger is not nearly so grave as the uncertainty experienced in dealing with the threats that lurk in the future for all mortal beings. Death casts a shadow over life, and this shadow becomes ever more difficult to ignore as the years accumulate. Even those fortunate ones whose lives have been filled with love and success will find great difficulty in accepting a future that seems dominated by frustration and death.

It is for this reason that faith in a transcendent and loving God is the only ultimately solid basis for the kind of trust that can survive all assaults. When trust faces the future, it becomes hope, and hope is valid ultimately only on the basis of God's promises. For it is only the promises of a divine being, who transcends history and mortality, that can be totally and finally trustworthy. And it is precisely this divine being who has been revealed in Christ and whose love, experienced in faith, can become a basis for trusting in the face of even the most frightening threats.

Therefore, just as trusting always requires an experience of being loved, so does ultimate trusting depend upon the experience of being loved by a God whose promises are valid beyond sickness and death. When we spoke, in Chapter 4, about the love of the hidden God made manifest and experienced in Christ, we were noting already the only source of trust that can deal with *all* the threats in life and in the future. For trust can develop only where there is experienced goodness, and there can be no experienced goodness quite like that of the divine love for us which we find in Christ Jesus. We can trust the future, therefore, not because we are strong or resourceful, but because it is in the keeping of one who loves us.

MONASTIC WITNESS IS CENTERED IN HOPE

When Benedict says in the Rule, "Place your hope in God alone" (RB 4:41), he is certainly referring to that hope which is impervious to all the assaults of distrust and despair. This is the trust in God that Benedict celebrated with his community when, week in and week out, they sang those words of Psalm 56: "...when I am afraid, I put my trust in you. In God, whose word I praise, in God I trust; I am not afraid; what can flesh do to me?" (vv. 3-4). The "word" that the psalmist praises represents all the promises of God, summed up in the essence of the covenant: "And I will walk among you, and will be your God, and you shall be my people" (Lev 26:12). Because of these promises, the believing Israelites knew that all the power of God was available to his faithful servants: "This I know, that God is for me" (Ps 56:9).

If the Israelites could be convinced of God's goodness and protection because of the covenant promises, Christian believers should be even more sure of this divine comfort as they become one with Christ who is the very embodiment of God's love for all humanity. The Word of God who is Christ is in fact a summary and reaffirmation of all the wonderful promises given to Israel. All those precious promises that were first given to Abraham and then passed down to us by the sure hands of believers have been validated in the most dramatic way in the person of Christ.

When St. Paul seeks to assure the rather suspicious Corinthians that he is not fickle or vacillating, he appeals to the primary model of faithfulness which is Christ himself. "As surely as God is faithful, our word to you has not been 'Yes and No.' For the Son of God, Jesus Christ, whom we proclaimed among you...was not 'Yes and No'; but in him it is always 'Yes.' *For in him every one of God's promises is a 'Yes.'* For this reason it is through him that we say the 'Amen,' to the glory of God" (2 Cor 1:18-20) (emphasis added). The believer's "Amen" thus recognizes and celebrates the utter trustworthiness of God as revealed and confirmed in Jesus. Benedict can counsel his followers to place their hope in God alone because Jesus has confirmed forever the utter trustworthiness of God.

REAL FAITH GOES DEEPER THAN WORDS

It is easy to forget that one's experience of God's utter trustworthiness does not come from saying "Amen" to a credal summary of true statements about God. Christians do not believe in magic. Rather, such a conviction derives from the experience of knowing the love of God in one's union with Christ. The statements of the creed serve as apt expressions of the implications of such union, but they are at best only a means by which the gift of faith is offered and embraced and increased.

We all know people whose words about faith are very accurate but whose attitudes toward life are negative and suspicious. This is proof that something more than words is required. In fact, since the attitudes of such people cancel all that their faith professes, it is clear that true orthodoxy is found first in one's interpretation of life and then only in one's words. For true faith always leads to hope, and such hope always expresses itself in a positive and trusting attitude toward life and people and the future.

It is in this context that we should read the celebrated description of faith in the letter to the Hebrews: "Now faith is the assurance of things hoped for, the conviction of things not seen" (11:1). The Greek word here translated as "assurance" means literally an "undergirding" or a "solid foundation." We have already noted that faith is a discovery of the goodness that God has hidden in life and, ultimately, in that deepest mystery which is the divine being. To the exact extent that faith enables one to be sure of that goodness, no more and no less, it is possible to face the future with courage and equanimity.

The author of Hebrews goes on then to show how that is

exactly what faith accomplished in the lives of the great believers of Israel. "By faith Abel offered to God a more acceptable sacrifice than Cain's....By faith Enoch was taken so that he did not experience death....By faith Noah, warned by God about events as yet unseen, respected the warning and built an ark to save his household....By faith Abraham obeyed when he was called to set out for a place that he was to receive as an inheritance....By faith he received power of procreation, even though he was too old—and Sarah herself was barren—because he considered him faithful who had promised" (Heb 11:4, 5, 7, 8, 11). Thus, it is clear that real faith changes people's lives and does not merely shape their creeds.

MONASTIC PROFESSION IS AN ACT OF FAITH

One finds everywhere in the Rule of Benedict evidence of such a positive attitude toward life and toward the future. Otherwise, he could never have described the monastic experience as a running toward the future "with inexpressible delight of love" (Prol 49). But there is perhaps no text in the Rule that expresses Benedict's trust in the future more than those words which he borrows from the psalmist and puts on the lips of the novice who is ready to begin the monastic journey of conversion. The ritual is solemn. After having placed the handwritten copy of his vows on the altar, "the novice himself begins the verse: 'Receive me, Lord, as you have promised, and I shall live; do not disappoint me in my hope' (Ps 119:116). The whole community repeats the verse three times, and adds 'Glory be to the Father.' Then the novice prostrates himself at the feet of each monk to ask his prayers, and from that very day, he is to be counted as one of the community" (RB 58:21-23).

This formula has been retained in monastic professions until the present day, and this fact alone should suffice to

show how profoundly monastic tradition has been influenced by the outlook of the scriptures. For it is a glimpse of
God's transcendent promise that has brought the candidate
to this threshold of monastic conversion. That promise was
seen in God's covenantal commitment to Israel and has
been brought to perfection in the person of Jesus. For he has
become the very embodiment of God's loving call to make
the journey of faith, first as Christians, and then, for some,
as monastic witnesses.

We have already noted that one form of this divine invitation is that baptismal election expressed in the words:
You are my beloved child. To the extent that faith enables a
person to hear those words ever more clearly, confidence
and trust in God's goodness will grow and strengthen in a
way that will be more than adequate for dealing with any
and all assaults of fear or anxiety. For trust deals with an
unknown threat by relying on a goodness that has been
known and experienced.

An example will illustrate the point. I recall vividly how
my niece, Clare Ann, could scarcely wait to begin school as
a six-year-old. However, after just two days of school she
was already convinced that it was not going to be as much
fun as she had anticipated. She locked herself in the bath-
room when it came time to catch the school bus. After her
mother pleaded with her, she finally emerged, snatched up
her book bag and, before slamming the door, said in a
rather loud voice: "Now, what about all that love...and
stuff?" She knew, of course, that her parents really did love
her, but she was confused, not being able to understand
why those who loved her would make her do something
that seemed opposed to her happiness. When her remem-
brance of past experiences of love won out over her present
doubts and fears, she had learned the meaning of trust.

When new monastics ask to be received and supported
in accordance with God's promise, they are also recalling

past experiences of God's goodness and can therefore pledge fidelity to a future that is unknown and will certainly be threatening at times. As those threats become more real and loom ever larger on the horizons of life, monastics will need to rely on all the hints and signs of goodness that have been offered. These will come from friends, from the goodness of life and directly from the experience of God's presence. It will be critically important that they learn how to pick these flowers and be strengthened by these angelic visits. Knowing how to receive and remember goodness is, in fact, the best way to prepare for trusting when goodness seems absent.

TRUST LIBERATES US FROM THE NEED TO CONTROL

One of the major reasons for our difficulties in becoming trusting people is our deep desire to control our lives. Our culture reinforces this and suggests that control is the only path to true happiness. Nothing could be farther from the truth. And this conclusion is a primary given of biblical and monastic wisdom. Such control is usually sought through the use of power, physical or psychic. However, a more subtle, but very real, form of control derives also from the acquisition and use of knowledge. Many learned people have great difficulty with the loss of control implied in a faith-interpretation of life. They find it very difficult to accept what they do not understand, forgetting that the best things in life are never fully understood.

The real blessings in life are gifts, and gifts are by definition beyond control. This is one of the realities of life that can be accepted only by the humble and the truly wise. Once again, we must remember that humility, as understood in the biblical and monastic traditions, coexists easily with a confidence based on God's goodness. But it is diametrically opposed to the illusion of autonomy and control.

Benedict makes it quite clear in chapter 7 that humility is a matter of recognizing the reality of one's human tendency to prideful thoughts and selfish desires (RB 7:14-25.31). Such a recognition is a pre-condition for seeking God's help. Obedience also is a natural expression of humility because it helps one to recognize and to reject the illusion and ultimate disappointment that come with a false sense of autonomy (RB 7:34-35).

This is the profound wisdom taught by Jesus in the first beatitude. For when he said, "Blessed are you who are poor, for yours is the kingdom of God" (Lk 6:20), he was not extolling the sad condition of physical poverty or destitution. Rather, he was declaring fortunate those who have discovered and accepted the reality of their powerless condition without God. The kingdom is given to them because they know that they do not control anything that is really important and are therefore free to turn to a loving God for all that matters in this life and in the future. Only those who accept the truth about their helpless condition without God can really expect salvation.

The same message is found in that dramatic and challenging statement of Jesus that "...unless you change and become like children, you will never enter the kingdom of heaven" (Mt 18:3). This does not mean that the condition for gaining heaven is to recover somehow a childlike innocence. Rather, it means to imitate a child's recognition of its own helpless condition and its consequent decision to rely on its parents in love and trust. In this context, then, "to change" means to turn *away* from the convenient but fatal illusion that one can really control the truly important things in life, like love and happiness. It means to turn *to* a loving God with well-founded trust that these gifts will be provided for those whose relationship with God is good and faithful.

The text in Matthew continues: "Whoever becomes

humble like this child is the greatest in the kingdom of heaven" (18:4). To be humble, therefore, means to live according to the truth that all good gifts come ultimately to those who trust in God's goodness rather than in their own resources. This does not mean, of course, that personal gifts are not to be cherished and developed. However, such development of one's natural talents will be a wholesome experience only if it happens in the context of one's recognition of the importance of God's grace in one's life. The alternative is the sad spectacle of an accomplished but proud and unpleasant personality.

Trust is based, therefore, on that radical humility which accepts simultaneously both a creature's powerlessness *and* the readiness of the creator to offer love and support. Surely it must have been this awareness that caused Paul to make that profound and paradoxical statement: "...whenever I am weak, then I am strong" (2 Cor 12:10). For if Paul is weak in a deceptive self-reliance it is only so that he can put all his trust in the power of God which he knows is available because of God's love for him.

NO REAL OBEDIENCE WITHOUT TRUST

This understanding of humility casts light also on Benedict's association of obedience with humility. He writes in chapter 7: "The third degree of humility is that a man submit to his superior in all obedience for the love of God, imitating the Lord of whom the Apostle says: 'He became obedient even to death' (Phil 2:8)" (RB 7:34). At first glance, it may seem that Benedict is simply saying that one must *endure* obedience as a fitting asceticism for one who knows his sinfulness. However, when we look at the example of Christ whom the monk is said to be imitating, it becomes quite clear that it is a matter of *trusting* the goodness of God even when that goodness demands something that is contrary to one's own preference or plan. Christ heard God call him his beloved Son and, in the freedom of that wonderful affirmation, he chose to trust God's will even when it meant an early and painful death.

Monastics too accept the guidance of obedience because they have come to see that this is necessary for effectively combating selfishness and for making a safe journey to that final home that divine love has promised. From this perspective, then, obedience, far from being something merely endured, becomes a guidance gladly accepted, because one trusts God as well as the superior who acts in God's name. This is true even when that goodness is wrapped in impenetrable mystery just as the passion of Jesus was a gift wrapped in the awful mystery of crucifixion.

If the monastic is supposed to be, like Jesus, "obedient even to death," it is important to look carefully at what really happened in the Lord's passion and death. When I wrote an earlier book on biblical spirituality (*Flowers in the Desert*), I knew that the last chapter would be on the resurrection as the homecoming of Jesus. But I wondered how the passion story could be related to homecoming. Then it suddenly dawned on me that it should be seen as a final and painful "letting go" of all previous wishes and plans so that the will of the divine Father could be perfectly realized. Accordingly, the chapter on the passion of Christ is entitled simply, "Letting Go."

Jesus let go of all his own plans and expectations when he said in Gethsemane, "not what I want, but what you want" (Mk 14:36). He did so because he trusted implicitly the goodness and love of the heavenly Father. Monastics also let go of their own judgments and plans when they put themselves under the guidance of a superior who represents the wisdom and goodness of the God whom they have come to trust. This can be a painful experience, as was the passion of Jesus. It can also be wonderfully fruitful.

Benedict recognized this when he wrote: "Never swerving from (God's) instructions, then, but faithfully observing his teaching in the monastery until death, we shall through patience share in the sufferings of Christ that we may deserve also to share in his kingdom" (Prol 50). The "instructions" and "teaching" of God in this passage are undoubtedly the scriptures as interpreted in the church and applied to the life of monastics by their superiors.

Moreover, this obedience, based on a radical trust in God and experienced as a letting go of all one's plans and expectations, will be required of all human beings when God calls them to that final journey into resurrection life. When it becomes evident that their illness is terminal, they will sense their union with Jesus in his final hours. Having been obedient and trusting in the days of their strength, they will know how to be so at the final moment as well.

Indeed, Jesus' acceptance of his heavenly Father's will in the garden of Gethsemane represented in a very real sense the climax of his passion. By comparison, the trials and the scourging and even the crucifixion were anticlimactic. The decisive moment had already occurred hours earlier when Jesus accepted his destiny. And that obedience in the garden was only the last of many acts of obedience during his ministry. The trust that makes obedience possible is not acquired in a day.

It would seem to follow that all Christians, monastic or otherwise, who learn to permit the revision or even the defeat of cherished plans because God has other plans for them will be preparing for their final obedience, which will be experienced then, not as a terrible surprise, but as something quite homogeneous with their previous life. Benedict makes this explicit for his followers when he speaks of faithful observance of God's teaching and patient sharing in the sufferings of Christ (Prol 50).

TRUST AND THE MYSTERY OF SUFFERING

When one sees human suffering in the context of trust and obedience, it is possible to approach in a new way the very difficult problem of the meaning of suffering in human life. We know that the suffering of Jesus was effective for our salvation because it came from his loving. Only that suffering of ours that comes from our loving can, therefore, be associated with the suffering of Jesus. There are many other kinds of suffering but they have little real value for salvation. This is especially true of suffering that comes from stubbornness or from a clinging to false goals. Such suffering may be intense but it has no relationship to the suffering of Jesus.

The "good" suffering that comes from loving is usually experienced when we put aside our plans for the sake of those we love. Such would be the case, for example, when parents give up vacation plans or make other sacrifices in order to provide a good education for their children. In such cases, one can actually see the benefit of the sacrifice. However, the suffering of innocent children, or of victims of war and natural disasters, or the patient suffering of old persons in nursing homes is more difficult to understand because it does not seem to serve any recognizable purpose.

This very real suffering can make some kind of sense, however, when it is accepted for love of God, that is, in a trusting spirit. For it is God, as lord of history, who disposes all things in ways that will ultimately serve divine justice and goodness as well as our own ultimate happiness. It is also God's prerogative to determine when we shall die. When we take such matters into our own hands, we show a lack of trust in God whose goodness during our lives should be a basis for trusting the divine decision about the end of life. This too is an obedience "for the love of God" (RB 7:34).

POVERTY

It is also in the context of a monastic person's trust in God that we should look for the meaning of monastic poverty. Benedict's concept of poverty has nothing in common with a love of destitution or a cultivated shabbiness. His words on this subject are quite clear: "A monk discovered with anything not given him by the abbot must be subjected to very severe punishment. In order that this vice of private ownership be completely uprooted, the abbot is to provide all things necessary...In this way every excuse of lacking some necessity will be taken away" (RB 55:17-19).

What is remarkable about this passage is the remedy that Benedict suggests for the preservation of a spirit of poverty in the monastery. He does indeed say that the offending monk should be disciplined. However, this solution deals only with a symptom of the deeper problem. Poverty is in real jeopardy when monastics lose their trust in the goodness and concern of the superior and therefore begin to hoard goods against a rainy day. The real problem is a lack of trust. This may be the fault of the superior but it is just as likely to be the result of a monastic's distrustful spirit.

Monastic poverty can easily be misunderstood or even caricatured. It has nothing to do with scruffy appearances. People who turn off lights in stairwells or who wear clothing beyond their intended usefulness may need counseling but they are scarcely exemplars of authentic poverty. The true meaning of monastic poverty is expressed beautifully in the gospel parables about the detachment that occurs when one has found an unexpected treasure.

In the words of Jesus, "The kingdom of heaven is like treasure hidden in a field, which someone found and hid; then in his joy he goes and sells all that he has and buys that field. Again, the kingdom of heaven is like a merchant in search of fine pearls; on finding one pearl of great value, he went and sold all that he had and bought it" (Mt 13:44-46). It must be assumed that the man who found the treasure and the merchant seeking pearls were both attached to their meager possessions until they found something far more precious. Suddenly, they are quite indifferent about possessions which had formerly seemed indispensable.

True monastic poverty is not, therefore, something sought for its own sake. Rather, it is a consequence of having become so rich in the discovery of God's goodness in one's life that one can afford to be poor and detached in every other way. Where one's faith has not in fact discovered that divine goodness, where one has not heard God calling him or her a beloved child, it will be quite impossible to be really detached from the security that possessions seem to offer. Moreover, in a culture that prizes possessions as the measure of one's worth, there is a constant danger of losing one's trust in God and reverting to an amassing of possessions as a proof of one's success or as an apparent source of security.

In this regard, Benedict joins the earlier monastic tradition in finding the ideal of poverty expressed in the attitudes of that first Jerusalem community described in the Acts of the Apostles. Those Christians, still living in the afterglow of the resurrection, manifested a carefree attitude about the goods of this world because they trusted God's goodness as it was made manifest in the kindness and care of their leaders and fellow believers.

Benedict wants monastic superiors to recognize their responsibility to be agents of that goodness. "The abbot must always bear in mind what is said in the Acts of the Apostles: 'Distribution was made to each one as he had need' (4:35)" (RB 55:20). The superior's responsibility to make concrete the goodness of God is paralleled by a corresponding responsibility of monastics to rely on the superior's care for all their legitimate needs. "For their needs (the monks) are to look to the father of the monastery, and are not allowed anything which the abbot has not given or permitted" (RB 33:5).

TRUST ILLUMINATES THE FUTURE

In the larger scheme of things, this trust in the goodness of the superior to provide for daily needs reflects a more basic trust in the goodness of God to provide abundantly for the community's ultimate needs. Since these ultimate needs pertain to the radical future, monastics will gradually put aside the comfort that comes from remembering past accomplishments and will begin to rely more and more on the promises of God to be realized as the future unfolds. Thus, the land of darkness and threat will become a land of light and promise.

Cardinal Newman, who seems to have been in some ways a secret Benedictine, expresses this in his somewhat romantic but still basically accurate depiction of monastic existence. "To the monk heaven was next door; he formed no plans, he had no cares; the ravens of his father Benedict were ever at his side. He 'went forth' in his youth 'to his work and his labor' until the evening of life; if he lived a day longer, he did a day's work more; whether he lived many days or few, he labored on to the end of them. He had no wish to see further in advance of his journey than where he was to make his next stage. He ploughed and sowed, he prayed, he meditated, he wrote, he taught, and then he died and went to heaven" ("The Mission of St. Benedict" in *Historical Sketches* II, pp. 426-27).

Such an idyllic picture is reminiscent of the community at Jerusalem: "All who believed were together and had all things in common; they would sell their possessions and goods and distribute the proceeds to all, as any had need" (Acts 2:44-45). The monastics described by Newman and the early Christians of Acts lived the spirit of poverty for one reason alone: because they trusted God's goodness in a community where that goodness was made available to all.

Just as monastics are expected to have a trusting attitude toward their superior, so also must the superior trust the good intentions and good will of the community members. The alternative is to be suspicious and defensive, always expecting and preparing for the worst. Superiors may sometimes feel betrayed by the lack of respect and responsiveness among community members. Benedict is careful to warn against such a tendency. "Excitable, anxious, extreme, obstinate, jealous or oversuspicious (the abbot) must never be. Such a man is never at rest" (RB 64:16). Trusting is always a risky business, but that is only because it is a primary fruit of real loving which always brings with it a vulnerability that may lead to severe pain but which is still infinitely better than the disappointment that awaits the person who chooses not to love.

KEEPING THINGS IN PERSPECTIVE

Finally, a positive and trusting spirit liberates a person to acquire that hallmark of the true believer which is a sense of humor. Humor is said to imply a certain incongruity, and it is hard to imagine anything more delightfully incongruous than finding peace and happiness in the midst of uncertainty and loss of control. Those who do not really trust God or the ultimate victory of God's love have little choice but to be grim and humorless. For they feel that they must assume all the responsibility for security in the world or orthodoxy in the church. True faith rejects the need to see everything in black-and-white clarity; it can be happy with gray areas of ambiguity or mystery. It rejects, therefore, that fundamentalist tendency which is found in all religions and which represents a bankruptcy of true and effective faith.

We have said that the firstfruits of one's discovery of the goodness of God is an indomitable trust—in God, in the future and in the good will of other persons. In the monastery, this will counteract the tendency to avarice and promote an authentic spirit of poverty. Hope will color everything and the future will be changed from a place of dread to a horizon illuminated by God's promises. Tradition has made Benedict the patron of a happy death. This surely reflects his confidence, reflected everywhere in the Rule, about the victory of divine promise in a life beyond death.

7

Compassion

*"(The abbot) is to imitate the example of
the good shepherd"* (RB 27:8).

Just as a deep sense of trust derives from the experience
of God's goodness in Christ, so also does compassion represent the flow of that divine goodness through believers to
benefit all those whom they touch. Benedict centers this
compassion in the person of the abbot who thereby takes on
the role of Christ as the good shepherd (Jn 10:1-18). All
other members of the monastic community, in accordance
with their responsibilities and to the degree of their union
with Christ, will also be able to channel this compassion for
the benefit of all.

THE ABBOT: PRIMARY AGENT OF COMPASSION

If there is anything clear in the Rule of Benedict, it is the
central role of the abbot. As superior, the abbot is responsible for everything in the monastery and will have to render an account to God for the health and happiness of the
community. "The abbot must, therefore, be aware that the
shepherd will bear the blame wherever the father of the
household finds that the sheep have yielded no profit" (RB
2:7). In fairness, Benedict goes on to point out that lack of
profit may indeed be due to the recalcitrance of the mem-

bers, in which case the abbot is to be exonerated from blame (RB 2:8-9). However, the abbot cannot easily assume that such is the case.

The primary duty of the abbot is, therefore, to assure that the goodness of God, as loving Father, is made present in the monastery in a truly effective manner. "To be worthy of the task of governing a monastery, the abbot must always remember what his title signifies and act as a superior should. He is believed to hold the place of Christ in the monastery, since he is addressed by a title of Christ, as the Apostle indicates: 'You have received the spirit of adoption as sons by which we exclaim, Abba, Father' (Rom 8:15)" (RB 2:1-3).

We have already commented on Benedict's surprising use of this text from Romans in reference to the role of Christ and, therefore, of the abbot. Benedict's assignment of a fathering role to Christ, in concert with earlier monastic tradition, may be due in part to their common stress on the divinity of Christ. However, the primary reason for this rather unconventional trinitarian theology seems to be Benedict's recognition that Christ is the one who makes the fathering love of God available in our world. Since we know and experience the Father's love only in Christ, it is easy to blur the distinction on the personal and experiential level. (This is, of course, also a mothering love but Benedict follows the lead of scripture in this regard.) What is really important here is the insistence that God's love is made available to us in Christ and that the abbot is the primary representative of this love in the monastery.

As we pointed out in Chapter 5, making God's love effectively available in the world is the primary role of Christ, and it is the love of Christ that works through believers to achieve this purpose. In a very real sense, believers love with the love of Christ in whom they now exist. Benedict seems to be saying nothing less than this when he declares that the abbot "is believed to hold the place of Christ in the monastery" (RB 2:2). This is very strong language. It cannot mean that the abbot somehow replaces Christ. But it does mean a lot more than being simply a representative of Christ. In fact, the abbot will be able to fulfill his demanding ministry of love and service only because the love of Christ works through him in a way that greatly enhances his own human capacity for loving.

GOD'S LOVING KINDNESS

It is evident everywhere in scripture that this divine loving is experienced first of all as compassion and mercy. In the Hebrew scriptures, this attribute of God is called *hesed*, which is usually translated as "loving kindness." The Lord will never be indifferent to sin, but there is a clear preference for divine mercy over justice. The divine predilection for mercy is expressed in many biblical passages. A typical example of this is found in Psalm 103: "The Lord is merciful and gracious, slow to anger and abounding in steadfast love *(hesed)*" (v. 8).

This reflects the powerful covenant commitment made by God to Moses: "The Lord passed before him, and proclaimed, 'The Lord, the Lord, a God merciful and gracious, slow to anger, and abounding in steadfast love and faithfulness, keeping steadfast love for the thousandth generation, forgiving iniquity and transgression and sin, yet by no means clearing the guilty...'" (Ex 34:6-7). In this passage, loving kindness is paired with the divine attribute of faithfulness, which suggests a love that survives betrayal and remains consistent and reliable in every circumstance.

The gospel of John recognizes these two divine qualities fully revealed in the incarnate Word: "And the Word became flesh and lived among us, and we have seen his glory, the glory as of a Father's only Son, full of grace and truth" (1:14). The "grace and truth" of this text are nothing less than the loving kindness and faithfulness of God in the Hebrew scriptures. And Jesus is that divine loving kindness and faithfulness now made incarnate in our world.

IMITATING THE GOOD SHEPHERD

It is precisely this combination of compassion and constancy that one finds expressed in Benedict's description of the abbot's role. He will show compassion by imitating the good shepherd. In fact, he strengthens the scriptural passage by laying special emphasis on the weakness and helplessness of the lost sheep. "(The abbot) is to imitate the example of the Good Shepherd who left the ninety-nine sheep in the mountains and went in search of the one sheep that had strayed. So great was his compassion for its weakness that he mercifully placed it on his sacred shoulders and so carried it back to the flock" (RB 27:8-9).

It is no easy task to aspire to the level of compassion represented in the model of the good shepherd. Small wonder, then, that Benedict reminds the abbot of this fact in no uncertain terms: "The abbot must always remember what he is and remember what he is called, aware that more will be expected of a man to whom more has been entrusted" (RB 2:30). When the abbot is aware of "what he is," he realizes that he is the primary exponent of God's love in the monastery; and when he remembers "what he is called," he hears an echo of those words of Benedict describing himself as "a father who loves you" (Prol 2).

Such a heavy responsibility seems less daunting when monastic superiors recall that, if more is required of them, it is only because they have also been blest with a generous measure of that divine love offered to us in Christ. In a word, to them more than to most are addressed those life-giving baptismal words by which we, like Jesus, are called God's beloved children.

Because superiors are so rich in God's love for them, they can afford to be generous and fair in their distribution of that love in the community. They will be imitating the gracious God of Israel's covenant, and will be fulfilling the ideal of the letter of James (2:13), by following the lead of a God for whom "mercy triumphs over judgment" (RB 64:10). This deep-seated preference for mercy will enable them to deal firmly with faults without being harsh or vindictive.

In this matter, Benedict is profoundly influenced by the model of the suffering servant of Isaiah and by Matthew's recognition of this ideal in the gentleness of Jesus. He reminds the abbot that "He must hate faults but love the brothers. When he must punish them, he must use prudence and avoid extremes; otherwise, by rubbing too hard to remove the rust, he may break the vessel. He is to distrust his own frailty and remember 'not to crush the bruised reed' (Is 42:3; Mt 12:20). By this we do not mean that he should allow faults to flourish, but rather, as we have already said, he should prune them away with prudence and love as he sees best for each individual" (RB 64:11-14). It must be obvious to all the community members that mercy is the superior's primary concern. If it is, he or she will be "loved rather than feared" (RB 64:15).

COMPASSION BEGINS WITH FAIRNESS

We have already noted that this divine kind of loving, mediated by the superior, derives from the goodness of the one loving rather than from the attractiveness of the one loved. When superiors love their communities in this way, they will carefully avoid the ever-present temptation to play favorites. This is such a serious matter because it undermines the community's trust in the superior's fairness. Benedict is forceful on this point: "The abbot should avoid all favoritism in the monastery. He is not to love one more than another unless he finds someone better in good actions and obedience" (RB 2:16-17). In other words, any signs of preference must be for reasons that are obvious to the whole community.

The superior may indeed reward goodness in the community members. The point is that such reward must be based on objective merit and not upon the superior's personal inclination. Benedict makes this quite clear when he writes: "Therefore, the abbot is to show equal love to everyone and apply the same discipline to all according to their merits" (RB 2:22).

If monastic superiors are to treat the members of their communities fairly, they must take the trouble to know them as individuals. They must know the color of their eyes, the dreams in their minds, and the fears or joys in their hearts. What separated the all-powerful God of Israel from the powerful pharaoh of Egypt was not the degree of their power but the way in which they viewed the Hebrew slaves. For the pharaoh, they were merely useful instruments of production; for God, they were chosen and beloved persons, with names and not just numbers. The pharaoh lost interest in them when they were too sick or old to work; God loves them forever.

When Benedict asks the superior to emulate the compassion of the good shepherd, he is asking nothing less than an imitation of that liberating love of the God of the exodus. When superiors show concern for individual community members, it will ensure that they not only know them well but will also be able to adapt the requirements of the Rule to their individual capabilities. Benedict warns the abbot that such meticulous concern will be difficult, but he does not soften his insistence that the abbot strive constantly to attain this ideal.

"In his teaching, the abbot should always observe the Apostle's recommendation, in which he says: 'Use argument, appeal, reproof' (2 Tm 4:2). This means that he must vary with circumstances, threatening and coaxing by turns, stern as a taskmaster, devoted and tender as only a father can be. With the undisciplined and restless, he will use firm argument; with the obedient and docile and patient, he will appeal for greater virtue; but as for the negligent and disdainful, we charge him to use reproof and rebuke" (RB 2:23-25).

Benedict does not hesitate to be repetitious in this important matter. Later in the same chapter, he writes: "(The abbot) must know what a difficult and demanding burden he has undertaken: directing souls and serving a variety of temperaments, coaxing, reproving and encouraging them as appropriate. He must so accommodate and adapt himself to each one's character and intelligence that he will not only keep the flock entrusted to his care from dwindling, but will rejoice in the increase of a good flock" (RB 2:31-32). Superiors will be able to bear such a "difficult and demanding burden" only if the love of God flows through them. For it is precisely this love of God in Christ, flowing out of the immense sea of divine goodness, that is able to comfort or challenge each person in accordance with his or her individual need and ability.

AN IDEAL OF GENTLENESS

It is this kind of loving that causes Benedict to insist in the most forceful language on the importance of care and concern for all those who are in need. He is gentle and patient beyond compare with those who are experiencing the fragility and weakness of the human condition. This is perhaps the single point on which Benedict parts company most decisively with his monastic predecessors. He espoused and taught a monastic ideal which was not restricted to physical and moral heroes. Rather, he ensured the perennial viability of this monastic ideal by making it something to which ordinary mortals could aspire.

Primary among such ordinary and fragile mortals are the sick and infirm members of the community. Benedict is explicit here: "Care of the sick must rank above and before all else, so that they may truly be served as Christ, for he said: 'I was sick and you visited me' (Mt 25:36), and, 'What you did for one of these least brothers you did for me' (Mt 25:40)" (RB 36:1-3). It is interesting to note that Benedict uses the same absolute language in regard to both the care of the sick and the place of Christ in the monastery (RB 4:21). Both are to be cherished before all else. This should not surprise us, because Benedict understood that Matthew's identification of Christ with all the needy ones made it clear that the love of God experienced in Christ is the same love that reaches out to the hungry and the thirsty and the homeless.

Benedict seems to have been pierced to the heart, in the sense of the desert fathers, by this Matthean parable of the last judgment. He refers to it twice, as noted above, in speaking about care for the sick. Likewise, among the Tools for Good Works, he lists: "'clothe the naked, visit the sick' (Mt 25:36)" (RB 4:15-16). Moreover, this is the leading biblical reference in his admonition concerning the monastery's attitude toward guests: "All guests who present themselves are to be welcomed as Christ, for he himself will say: 'I was a stranger and you welcomed me' (Mt 25:35)" (RB 53:1). Benedict seems to have understood perfectly the serious challenge of this passage for all who claim to be united with Christ but are tempted to ignore or neglect the needy persons in their midst.

SOLICITUDE FOR SINNERS

If it can be said that Benedict guided the monastic tradition toward a far more compassionate attitude in regard to the weak and the ailing, one must also note that his approach is even more revolutionary in regard to delinquent members of the monastic community. He seems to have understood that people who do wrong are not always acting out of malice or perversity but more frequently are psychically or morally wounded through fear or lack of love or low self-esteem. Accordingly, his approach is compassionate and medicinal rather than angry or vindictive.

Benedict is certainly not indifferent toward sinfulness or naive about its possibility. But he is exceedingly patient and loving in the way he deals with those who have committed sin. This is evident from that golden passage in chapter 28: "...the abbot should follow the procedure of a wise physician. After he has applied compresses, the ointment of encouragement, the medicine of divine Scripture, and finally the cauterizing iron of excommunication and strokes of the rod, and if he then perceives that his earnest efforts are unavailing, let him apply an even better remedy: he and all the brothers should pray for him so that the Lord, who can do all things, may bring about the health of the sick brother" (RB 28:2-5).

When one considers how easily superiors can feel angry and betrayed by the recalcitrance of their monastic charges, such a positive and hopeful attitude toward delinquent behavior is indeed remarkable. This demonstrates, more than anything else, the experience and wisdom of Benedict. It also reveals to what extent he felt affirmed by God's love and was able, therefore, to rise above feelings of personal hurt or resentment. As mentioned earlier, when one is rich in the experience of God's love, one can afford to react with patience and understanding to human failings.

It is precisely in this context of concern for delinquent monks that Benedict urges the abbot to follow the example of the good shepherd (RB 27:8-9). He sharpens this admonition by providing the contrasting example of the wicked shepherds described so vividly by Ezekiel: "Let (the abbot) also fear the threat of the Prophet in which God says: 'What you saw to be fat you claimed for yourselves, and what was weak you cast aside' (Ez 34:3-4)" (RB 27:7). And Benedict summarizes his views with a statement of chilling clarity: "(The abbot) should realize that he has undertaken care of the sick, not tyranny over the healthy" (RB 27:6).

COMPASSION FOR STRANGERS

Benedict asks the abbot to show compassion in a special way to guests and visitors to the monastery. Here again, he sees a real identification between Christ and those travel-weary ones who are drawn to the peace and security of the monastic environment. He makes this explicit in his chapter on the reception of guests: "All guests who present themselves are to be welcomed as Christ, for he himself will say: 'I was a stranger and you welcomed me' (Mt 25:35)" (RB 53:1).

Benedict is insistent about this identification of the guest with Christ. "All humility should be shown in addressing a guest on arrival or departure. By a bow of the head or by a complete prostration of the body, Christ is to be adored because he is indeed welcomed in them" (RB 53:6-7). And again, "Great care and concern are to be shown in receiving poor people and pilgrims, because in them more particularly Christ is received" (RB 53:15).

Anyone who has had experience with monastic guests will know how difficult it is to resist a tendency to be impatient or even callous when faced with a continuous stream of guests, at all hours of the day and late into the evening. Some of them have not made appropriate reservations and others are quite inconsiderate in their expectations. It will not be enough merely to think about Christ in one's efforts to be kind and thoughtful in their regard. It is only the love of God, experienced in Christ and flowing through the guestmaster, that will make it possible to respond faithfully to these admonitions of Benedict. The same is true of the patience and kindness required of all who deal with outsiders in the name of the community. Receptionists, telephone operators and others who deal constantly with visitors must bear some responsibility for creating an atmosphere of understanding and concern.

Because of the importance that Benedict attaches to the proper reception of guests, it has become customary to associate Benedictines with generous hospitality. But surely it must be evident that Benedictines do not enjoy a monopoly in this regard. After all, Franciscans and Dominicans and Jesuits, not to mention other religious, also honor the virtue of hospitality and are often exemplary in this respect.

If there is a special affinity of Benedictines for hospitality, it is probably due to their insistence on common prayer which they consider to be an entertainment of God's mysterious presence among them. The hospitality shown to guests is like that shown by Abraham and Sarah (Gn 18:1-15), who welcomed three strangers in their old age and thereby expressed their readiness to make room for God's mysterious plan in their lives. Indeed, it is those who gladly entertain divine mystery who will also be ready to make room for human strangers in their carefully ordered lives. More will be said about this when we speak of community prayer in Chapter 9.

EDUCATION WITH A HEART

Benedict also sees the abbot's love and compassion expressed in his role as the primary teacher in the monastic community. This is evident in the very first sentence of the Rule: "Listen carefully, my son, to the master's instructions, and attend to them with the ear of your heart" (Prol 1). From the context, it is clear that the abbot is not a master or teacher in the sense of one who is concerned only with providing knowledge in a disciplined environment. While such factors are not unimportant, the emphasis here is on the manner in which knowledge and wisdom are shared. It is love and compassion that prompt the abbot to make available to others the blessing of his experience and the revealed truth about how to find final happiness.

This teaching of the abbot is addressed to the heart of the monastic person. It is far more than a mere transfer of ideas. That is why the abbot's personal observance of the truth he communicates is so important. "…[A]nyone who receives the name of abbot is to lead his disciples by a twofold teaching: he must point out to them all that is good and holy more by example than by words, proposing the commandments of the Lord to receptive disciples with words, but demonstrating God's instructions to the stubborn and the dull by living example. Again, if he teaches his disciples that something is not to be done, then neither must he do it, 'lest after preaching to others, he himself be found reprobate' (1 Cor 9:27)" (RB 2:11-13).

Over the centuries since the time of Benedict, education has been a primary apostolate of monastics. In fact, it has been said, with only moderate exaggeration, that the monks and nuns taught Europe how to read and write. Where Benedictines have been successful in education, it has been due, not only to their competence, but especially to their ability to provide an atmosphere of respect and concern for students as individuals. And this is communicated as much by example as by precept. Hearing about respect and sensitivity is never enough; it must also be experienced.

PERSONAL INTEGRITY

Benedict has good reason to insist on the sincerity of the abbot and, indeed, of all who profess to lead the monastic life. Very few sins are condemned more consistently in the scriptures than the sin of false pretense. This kind of fault is particularly blameworthy in matters of religion where it becomes an attractive substitute for the difficult and painful process of true spiritual conversion. And since monastic life is based entirely upon the reality of personal conversion, such sham or pretense may be seen as the primary "occupational hazard" of professed religious.

Already in the Prologue, Benedict shows his concern for personal honesty and sincerity in prospective followers. He pictures the Lord summoning the monastic "workman" from the multitude of Christians and then observes: "If you hear this and your answer is 'I do,' God then directs these words to you: If you desire true and eternal life, 'keep your tongue free from vicious talk and your lips from all deceit...'(Ps 34:13)" (Prol 17).

And, a little later, he notes again the need to be rid of all forms of deceit. One who hopes to dwell in God's kingdom must note the conditions laid down by the Lord: "'One who walks without blemish,' he says, 'and is just in all his dealings; who speaks the truth from his heart and has not practiced deceit with his tongue...' (Ps 15:2-3)" (Prol 25-26). It may not always be possible to live entirely in harmony with the ideals that one professes. However, when the gap between professed belief and actual practice becomes too great, there will be a loss of personal integrity which cannot fail to undermine one's witness. To offer such a false coin is to be seriously lacking in love and compassion toward those whose trust is thus betrayed.

FIRST THINGS FIRST

A genuine love and compassion for community members will also guide the monastic superior toward a recognition of the priority of their spiritual welfare over all other considerations. The good works of the monastery are, after all, merely the by-product of its primary function as a place where men and women can be supported on their journey to their final homeland. We have already noted Benedict's great concern lest the abbot lay burdens on the monks without due consideration for their varying capacities. In many modern monasteries, the superior is an administrator with wide-ranging responsibilities. There will always be that temptation to overload the willing worker or, perhaps, to permit the workaholic to indulge his or her addiction without adequate warning.

Benedict could hardly be clearer on this subject: "Above all, (the abbot) must not show too great concern for the fleeting and temporal things of this world, neglecting or treating lightly the welfare of those entrusted to him. Rather, he should keep in mind that he has undertaken the care of souls for whom he must give an account. That he may not plead lack of resources as an excuse, he is to remember what is written: 'Seek first the kingdom of God and his justice, and all these things will be given you as well' (Mt 6:33), and again, 'Those who fear him lack nothing' (Ps 34:10)" (RB 2:33-36).

These biblical words have become so familiar that we may very well fail to see their full implications. When it is said that those who fear the Lord will lack nothing, it does not mean that they will have everything their hearts desire. Rather, having discovered the loving and comforting presence of God, they will lack nothing of any real importance. The goal of the monastic person is neither physical comfort nor destitution but rather a simplicity of life which is possible where God's presence is felt and appreciated.

AUTHORITY USED WITHOUT
COMPASSION IS TYRANNY

Everything that has been said about the love of God flowing through the abbot for the benefit of the community can be said of every person in the monastery in accordance with his or her responsibilities there. In most modern monasteries, this will apply first of all to the prior or second in command. For Benedict, however, the most important dispenser of compassion after the abbot is the cellarer. If the abbot is the heart of the monastery, the cellarer is its hands. For it is his duty to care for the thousand and one details that ensure the harmonious functioning of a complex community organism. (In modern monasteries, the cellarer's role is usually taken by the prior, with assistance from the business manager.)

Benedict is very clear about the nature and the parameters of the cellarer's responsibilities. This special person, who is entrusted with the daily needs of the monastic community, has a profound influence on the morale and happiness of the community. Small wonder, then, that Benedict defines his qualities with such care. "As cellarer of the monastery, there should be chosen from the community someone who is wise, mature in conduct, temperate, not an excessive eater, not proud, excitable, offensive, dilatory or wasteful, but God-fearing, and like a father to the whole community. He will take care of everything, but will do nothing without an order from the abbot" (RB 31:1-4).

What is remarkable about Benedict's description of the cellarer's office is the emphasis he places on the *manner* in which the responsibilities of that office are to be discharged. Not only must the cellarer be efficient and practical; he must also have a congenial and patient attitude. In our contemporary world, productivity and profit margin frequently become the sole considerations while the human side of the equation is ignored or sacrificed. For Benedictines, *how* a work is done is just as important as *that* it is done. A venerable and wise professor made this clear to me during my days as a student in Rome. Noting how impressed we students were with the monuments of imperial Rome, he warned us: Never forget that all these splendid monuments were built by the sweat and blood of slaves. Today we are tempted to admire successful business enterprises even when they ignore the legitimate needs of workers and their families. Benedict and his true followers will always put compassion ahead of efficiency.

Benedict's words in this regard speak for themselves: "(The cellarer) should not annoy the brothers. If any brother happens to make an unreasonable demand of him, he should not reject him with disdain and cause him distress, but reasonably and humbly deny the improper request....Above all, let him be humble. If goods are not available to meet a request, he will offer a kind word in reply, for it is written: A kind 'word is better than the best gift' (Sir 18:17)" (RB 31:6-7;13-14). How refreshing it is to hear that those in authority should not even annoy their charges. Too often it is just the other way around.

We must not fail to notice the radical nature of these admonitions. It is almost taken for granted in our society that, if one possesses some measure of authority or power, it is legitimate to let the petitioner know, in subtle but unmistakable ways, that a favor is being bestowed. This thinly disguised punishment for being needy has no place in a community where all should know that authority is a gift from God to be exercised with genuine humility and compassion. Moreover, what Benedict says about the cellarer applies to every single member of the community in accordance with his or her ability to show love and mercy.

LIVING UNDER A RULE

A special safeguard to ensure the appropriate use of power in the monastery is the existence of the Rule itself. Benedict gives the abbot extraordinary discretion but he also reminds him that he must always carry out his mandate within the limits of the Rule. In this way, the community has some protection against an arbitrary or whimsical use of authority. "(The abbot) must, above all, keep this rule in every particular..." (RB 64:20).

Since the Rule itself is an attempt to apply biblical wisdom to the monastic calling, Benedict wishes the abbot to be well aware of biblical teaching and to make it the basis of his own instructions. "(The abbot) ought, therefore, to be learned in divine law, so that he has a treasury of knowledge from which he can 'bring out what is new and what is old' (Mt 13:52)" (RB 64:9). Moreover, "the abbot must never teach or decree or command anything that would deviate from the Lord's instructions" (RB 2:4). Monastic superiors need not have a formal or academic knowledge of scripture or theology. Rather, they are to be so familiar with the wisdom of the scriptures that their whole system of values will be shaped by the biblical spirit.

Benedict's expectations of the monastic superior would seem to exceed the capacity of normal human beings. And that is why it is so important to realize that this kind of love and wisdom and compassion will always be possible only where God's love, experienced in Christ, flows through the superior to bless abundantly the members of the monastic community. Such compassion is indeed the firstfruits of the loving made possible through one's union with Christ.

Perceptive parents or others who exercise authority will

have no difficulty in recognizing the wisdom of Benedict expressed in these pages. In their situations also, mercy must be preferred to judgment, and the loving care of the good shepherd remains the perennial ideal. Moreover, the particular capacities and weaknesses of charges must always be taken into consideration. Sometimes we take resistance too personally and make little or no allowance for innocent mischief as young persons test the boundaries of their freedom. In all these areas, Benedict's words are precious.

8

Discipline

*"Therefore, they are eager to take
the narrow road"* (RB 5:11).

It is fitting that we should reflect on the role of discipline
in the monastery after having noted that Benedict is concerned first of all about trusting God's goodness and sharing that goodness through compassion. Just as God is said
to prefer mercy to justice, so does Benedict want the abbot
to be experienced as a loving father before he is known as a
stern legislator. There is much in the Rule about law and
sanctions and discipline but these are only means to a
higher end. They are all subordinate to the journey of personal conversion in the love of Christ.

DISCIPLINE SERVES LOVE

This is quite explicit in the Rule itself. Benedict writes:
"It is love that impels (monks) to pursue everlasting life;
therefore, they are eager to take the narrow road of which
the Lord says: 'Narrow is the road that leads to life' (Mt
7:14)" (RB 5:10-11). This road is certainly not chosen
because it is narrow but rather because it leads to the fulfillment of that vision which brought monastics to the
monastery in the first place and which remains the passion
of their lives. This "love that impels" is, therefore, nothing

less than the love of God appropriated by monastics through their union with Christ.

One of the primary duties of the monastic community is to reassure its younger members about the necessity and value of this "narrow road" which alone leads to the realization of their dreams. We recall the words of Benedict: "Do not be daunted immediately by fear and run away from the road that leads to salvation. It is bound to be narrow at the outset" (Prol 48). The older members of the community, by their witness of genuine concern and quiet joy, will strengthen the resolve of beginners. For they will hopefully see in these veterans of the struggle the fulfillment of that promise of Benedict that their hearts will eventually overflow "with the inexpressible delight of love" (Prol 49).

Benedict's understanding of the role of religious law is perfectly in harmony with the teaching of scripture on this subject. Already in Israel, Torah, which is more properly translated "instruction" than "law," was always intended as a guide for those who had already experienced goodness and wished to respond in love and gratitude. We have already noted the crucial importance of the preamble to the ten commandments which introduces Yahweh as the one who has delivered Israel from bondage and *therefore* offers the prescriptions that follow as important ways in which that freedom can be channeled into gratitude and correct moral behavior.

Law does not provide freedom; only love can do that. But law serves a useful purpose in directing freedom so that it will be used in accordance with God's purposes. According to the ten commandments, the first such purpose is to show due respect and gratitude to God who is the ultimate source of freedom. Magic and superstition are offensive to God because they attempt to manipulate one who has already demonstrated love and care. The other commandments deal with those precious and vulnerable gifts in life which are derived from God's gracious mystery. These are such basic things as life, love, good reputation, security and the peaceful enjoyment of one's blessings.

THE PROPER ROLE OF LAW

The law thus commands those who have received the precious gift of freedom to use it in a way that will make its blessings available to others. This requires respect for their mystery and a renunciation of violence in all its forms. When law is imposed where there is no freedom, it can only produce slavish compliance or, worse still, an increase of bondage in the form of guilt. Ironically and tragically, when law ceases to be a guide for love and freedom, it becomes instead a tyrant as destructive as any pharaoh.

The writings of St. Paul offer profound insights into this useful but limited role of law. Law is useful, first of all, because it challenges and exposes our powerless condition in matters of salvation. The law presented an ideal that could not be realized by human effort alone. In Paul's words: "I was once alive apart from the law, but when the commandment came, sin revived and I died, and the very commandment that promised life proved to be death to me" (Rom 7:9-10). One could say, in a sense, that the law provides a road-map but no fuel.

It is true, of course, that laws can be observed up to a point through mere human effort but the results are almost always vitiated by pride, leading to rash judgment and odious comparisons. There is no salvation on that road, for authentic salvation is always a gift of God and is given only to those who humbly acknowledge their need. Paul writes: "Then what becomes of boasting? It is excluded. By what law? By that of works? No, but by the law of faith. For we hold that a person is justified by faith apart from works prescribed by the law" (Rom 3:27-28). There is no salvation on the road of human effort and human boasting; salvation is always a gift of God and it is given only to those who humbly acknowledge their need.

The primary benefit of law is, therefore, its ability to guide the freedom which is God's gift. The gift of freedom received through love thus becomes a gift of loving service to others. In that case, there are, and must be, good works but they are really only by-products of the faith that saves. They also serve to make visible the reality of that faith. Thus, good works are the effect of saving faith and, accordingly, no cause for boasting.

It is important for monastics to pay attention to Paul's theology because, through their emphasis on ascetical practices, they have always been exposed to the charge of Pelagianism. Pelagius was himself a monk and it was his heresy of good works that Augustine confronted in his writings on grace. A careful reading of Benedict's Rule, however, makes it quite clear that he was a monk who understood Paul's theology and therefore saw clearly the correct role of law in the Christian economy of salvation. His emphasis on grace is evident in such statements as the following: "First of all, every time you begin a good work, you must pray to (God) most earnestly to bring it to perfection" (Prol 4). Or, again: "With (God's) good gifts which are in us, we must obey him at all times…" (Prol 6).

HUMILITY DELIVERS US FROM ILLUSION

Benedict's emphasis on humility is the solid basis of his orthodox teaching in this regard. As we have noted, he understood humility as an embracing of reality, and reality includes both our own helplessness and God's loving care. The apparent holiness that comes from human effort, relying solely on ascetical practices and good works, is in fact a dangerous *illusion*. But it is a very attractive illusion because it assures a reputation for holiness without the need to sacrifice one's pride. As such, it is no doubt the most dangerous temptation offered to those who strive for holiness.

As a wise and experienced spiritual master, Benedict certainly understood this danger. The whole purpose of monastic discipline, then, is to confront and expose those illusions which attack the very foundation of humility and therefore of genuine spirituality. It is painful to embrace reality because at the heart of it is the fact of one's powerless condition. True conversion requires monastics to let go of all those many and clever stratagems by which human beings try to control the sources of security and happiness. Such efforts, however valiant they may be, are entirely futile since real security and happiness are always a gift of God.

Monastic discipline is designed, therefore, to hold monastics to a life-situation in which it will be difficult to avoid the truth about their powerless condition before God. But the same community experience will hopefully also reveal the truth about God's boundless mercy which alone can turn that condition into a source of humility and love. Monastic discipline may indeed be opposed to indulgence but, long before that and at a much deeper level, it is opposed to evasion.

A SCHOOL FOR THE LORD'S SERVICE

This healthy situation which offers a solid foundation for spiritual growth in love is, in the words of Benedict, "a school for the Lord's service" (Prol 45). This is no academic institution; rather, it is a place where one can learn that which is most important for human beings, namely, how to serve the Lord and thus find the happiness which God intends for us all.

In establishing this special kind of school, Benedict recognizes the need for discipline, but it is not a discipline for its own sake or even for good order. Benedict writes: "In drawing up its regulations, we hope to set down nothing harsh, nothing burdensome. The good of all concerned, however, may prompt us to a little strictness in order to amend faults and to safeguard love" (Prol 46-47). Surely when Benedict says that discipline is justified in order to "amend faults," he includes the correction of those forms of self-delusion that find expression in pride and self-righteousness.

And how does one "safeguard love" more effectively than by embracing reality in humility and trust? For in this way one enters into that paradox of strength combined with vulnerability that becomes possible when one knows the presence and love of God in one's life. As one is gradually liberated from the false comfort of illusions and is made strong by the reality of God's love, it will be possible to make rapid progress on that journey of real conversion and ultimate joy that Benedict lays out before his followers.

We recall again those celebrated words: "Do not be daunted immediately by fear and run away from the road that leads to salvation. It is bound to be narrow at the outset. But as we progress in this way of life and in faith, we shall run the path of God's commandments, our hearts overflowing with the inexpressible delight of love" (Prol 48-49). Benedict clearly recognizes that fear is a serious problem for those beginning this journey. Illusions can be very persuasive in claiming to be indispensable for security and happiness. They have the power of an addiction. In the "school for the Lord's service," however, wise counseling and gentle encouragement will make it possible to abandon fear and to risk reliance on the goodness of God.

SOME VERY DANGEROUS ILLUSIONS

It is easy to identify some of the most common and most dangerous kinds of illusion. First of all, there is the illusion of *autonomy*. We all cherish our independence and we like to believe that we can be basically self-sufficient. In the modern western world, where famine is almost unknown, it is easier to maintain this illusion than in the world of the bible. If we have a little money and live near a supermarket and own a pet, we can survive almost indefinitely. But this is no real living, for there can be no human happiness except in the risk of giving and receiving. Creatures are by definition contingent beings. They need each other and, most of all, they need God. That is reality; all else is dangerous reverie.

Then there is the illusion of happiness through *control*. We feel that if we could just get our lives organized in such a way that there would be no surprises we would finally be happy. Those who live in this illusion want to analyze and understand everything. They have difficulty with the mysteries of faith. They are particularly disturbed by the unpredictability of God and of other free beings. Their friends tend to be people who usually agree with them and share their prejudices. But the real God is wildly unpredictable and the friends we should really want are those who tell us what we need to hear rather than what pleases us. To require control is to practice idolatry and to risk eternal boredom.

Another dangerous illusion is that of *immortality*. We all know, of course, that we will die. What we fail to note is that we are dying every day. Those who entertain this illusion are often living in denial. They refuse to check out suspicious physical or psychological symptoms, or to ask for help, because they desperately hope that problems will go away if they are ignored. This is a special danger for younger people. They take intolerable risks because they think that they are somehow immune from fatal consequences. I have often thought that rules and regulations for teenagers are intended simply to keep them alive long enough to discover what life is really all about.

Another common illusion is the fantasy that true growth can be achieved *without pain*. Our culture is incredibly fearful of pain. It must be eliminated at all cost and as soon as possible. But growing always involves an element of pain, for one cannot go forward without leaving something good behind. And one cannot truly love without the pain of sacrifice. Those who have an unhealthy fear of pain have great difficulty in making permanent commitments. They want to have the future without giving up any part of the past. They have not learned that one cannot open a door completely without closing some other doors completely. Pain, therefore, is part of life; it reminds us that we are alive, and there can be no successful living without it.

It should be noted also that dangerous illusions are probably found most commonly among very talented people. Since they are very good in one area, and are applauded for that, they are often unwilling to deal realistically with serious shortcomings in other parts of their lives. This is of particular significance for monasteries because the monastic life has often attracted the best and the brightest. What Benedict says about discipline should, therefore, be taken very seriously by monastics.

MONASTIC STABILITY

The importance of recognizing and dealing honestly with illusions in one's life accounts for Benedict's insistence on monastic stability. He makes it the subject of a special vow for his followers: "When (the novice) is to be received, he comes before the whole community in the oratory and promises stability, fidelity to monastic life, and obedience" (RB 58:17). The reason for this special emphasis on stability becomes clear when we notice what he says about the wandering monks of his day.

Benedict calls these wandering monks "gyrovagues,

who spend their entire lives drifting from region to region,
staying as guests for three or four days in different monasteries. Always on the move, they never settle down, and are
slaves to their own wills and gross appetites" (RB 1:10-11).
There was an honorable tradition of wandering monks as
witnesses to our pilgrim status in this world. But Benedict
recognized the serious danger in this nomadic existence
and he was convinced that the danger far outweighed the
witness value in such a freewheeling kind of life.

It should be obvious that our deep-seated shortcomings
are not likely to be discovered by looking in the mirror. We
become so adept at protecting and justifying such tendencies that it is only through consultation with other insight-
ful and honest persons that we have any hope of exposing
them. Benedict wants his followers to stay in one place,
where others can get to know them well, and where these
others will, in various ways, enable them to learn the truth
about themselves. This is a matter of critical importance
because real spiritual growth can only occur when one
begins with honest self-knowledge.

The various ways in which this can occur are, for example, good spiritual direction, the constructively critical
comments of one's superior and confreres as well as the
observations of good and honest friends. To leave the community as soon as the truth begins to hurt, claiming that
one's confreres are lacking in charity or understanding,
usually means taking the path of evasion and illusion. In a
sense, monastic stability can be compared to the need for a
sculptor to hold a block of marble firmly in place so that he
or she may effectively carve and shape it with the chisel.
The monastic too must stay in one place to be shaped and
formed by the chisel of truth.

The proper observance of monastic stability, then, is not
so much a matter of remaining physically in one place as it
is a willingness to hear the truth about oneself. This is really

to practice humility which, as we have noted, means embracing reality. Monastics may very well remain constantly in the monastery and still refuse to acknowledge the truth about their true condition before God. Therefore, stability has far more to do with honesty than it does with one's zip code.

PUNISHMENT FOR FAULTS

Anyone who reads the Rule will notice and may even be made uneasy by the amount of space that Benedict devotes to punishment for those who are disobedient or recalcitrant. It should also be noted, however, that he is much more lenient in this regard than most of his monastic predecessors. Moreover, he warns the abbot on several occasions to let compassion temper his sense of justice. He writes, for example, "The abbot must exercise the utmost care and concern for wayward brothers, because 'it is not the healthy who need a physician, but the sick' (Mt 9:12)" (RB 27:1).

It is interesting to note that, in this quotation from Matthew's gospel, Jesus is rejecting the criticism of the Pharisees, who think that he is being indifferent toward sin because he associates with sinners. We suspect, of course, that the Pharisees were sinners too, but Jesus could not help them because they refused to acknowledge their need. They lived in the illusion of a holiness based on external observance. It seems, in fact, that Jesus deliberately chose to work miracles on the sabbath in order to expose the lack of mercy in their piety. Benedict quotes this text because he wishes the abbot to imitate the mercy of Jesus and not the self-righteous and judgmental attitude of the Pharisees.

Among the various sanctions specified by Benedict, it may be particularly difficult for us to understand the penalty of excommunication. This is not a punishment that seems helpful in our modern society, partly because the fault to be corrected is often already a kind of self-excommunication. However, in Benedict's environment, this penalty was no doubt both appropriate and effective.

When one enters into the pattern or rhythm of a typical Benedictine community, the result is a real sense of support and security. There may be, however, a downside to this rhythmic existence. For the same community routine that creates comfort and enables one to deal with the uncertainties of life may also have an anesthetic or lulling effect. Serious personal faults or defects may thus be hidden under the cover of daily routine. In that case, observance as usual may actually make it more difficult to recognize and deal effectively with problems that need to be addressed. In such cases, excommunication becomes a kind of shock therapy to awaken the monastic to the seriousness of his or her situation. In cases where offending monastics no longer rely on community support, a gentle but firm reminder of the importance of personal integrity may be effective.

VOCATIONAL ROMANTICISM

Benedict's concern for the exposure and elimination of illusions in the lives of his followers is reflected also in his directives concerning the admission of candidates to the monastery. In these days, when we are inclined to produce glossy and enticing vocational literature and to lavish attention on potential candidates, we are a little shocked to read in the Rule: "Do not grant newcomers to the monastic life easy entry, but, as the Apostle says, 'Test the spirits to see if they are from God' (1 Jn 4:1)" (RB 58:1-2). In this reference to scripture, Benedict clearly shows his concern lest the candidate be motivated by reasons that are not at all in harmony with the ideals of the monastic life.

Nor may we assume that Benedict was simply cautioning against a careless and indiscriminate admission of novices.

For he goes on to spell out the serious testing that should confront a candidate. "Therefore, if someone comes and keeps knocking at the door, and if at the end of four or five days he has shown himself patient in bearing his harsh treatment and difficulty of entry, and he has persisted in his request, then he should be allowed to enter and stay in the guest quarters for a few days" (RB 58:3-4). Moreover, during the novitiate, "The novice should be clearly told all the hardships and difficulties that will lead him to God" (RB 58:8).

One should not be too quick to assume that Benedict was allowing himself a bit of rhetorical exaggeration here. Those who are experienced in the task of screening candidates for a monastery will be quick to recognize that Benedict is undoubtedly warning about the very real threat to monastic life posed by those who seek out monasteries, not for the hard task of personal conversion, but merely in order to indulge some romantic attraction to what they perceive to be the idyllic existence of daydreamers. In other words, Benedict wishes to deny entrance to those who make their monastic project nothing more than a studied entertainment of illusions.

HUMAN VERSUS DIVINE ORDER

We have already noted that Benedict did not insist on discipline primarily for the sake of good order in the monastery. This is a matter of some importance because it has become one of the conventional assumptions about Benedict's priorities. Almost every monastic must have heard at least once in homilies about Benedict that he was "the last of the Romans," and that he stood for law and order in the face of the chaos introduced by the hordes of barbarians that were sweeping over Italy in the sixth century. Though not without an element of truth, such an assumption about Benedict's concern for order is far too simplistic.

In this regard also Benedict certainly draws his wisdom from the scriptures. And when we look closely at scripture we note that there is a very important distinction drawn between the kind of order sought and cherished by humans and that which is the special order of the Holy Spirit. There is a human order which is not based on justice but which merely guarantees that those who enjoy large possessions will be allowed to keep them undisturbed. Thus, there was the vaunted neatness and good order of Egyptian civilization under the pharaohs. The problem is that it was an order that protected the elite and brought misery and oppression to the Hebrew slaves. In fact, this specious kind of order is usually promoted most assiduously in countries with totalitarian governments.

Human order is imposed by men for human purposes. And those who clamor for "law and order" usually have this kind of order in mind. But there is the order of the Spirit also. This order is far more concerned with justice and equity than with peaceful appearances. This kind of order seeks to provide not only for the elite, but for everyone without distinction. Since it is far more difficult to provide for all, and not just for a few, this kind of order often cannot afford to be neat or meticulous. But it has the great advantage of being the beautiful order intended by God from the beginning of creation.

When we notice how careful Benedict is to take into consideration the special circumstances of every single individual, we see immediately that he too is seeking an order and harmony in the monastery that reflects the divine order of justice and compassion revealed in the scriptures. There is a value in external order and Benedict certainly recognized that. Otherwise, he would not have been so concerned about such matters as sounding the bell at the proper time for prayer (RB 11:12-13). But this order is totally subordinate to the order of justice and compassion and love.

Parents often find it hard to determine what kind of discipline is appropriate in the difficult task of rearing children. If they adopt the wisdom of Benedict, they will be guided by their love and will avoid both the authoritarian model which produces frightened or rebellious children and the indulgent model which is a flight from responsibility. There should be enough freedom to permit some innocent mischief, as children probe the boundaries of their freedom. When I was in charge of discipline in our seminary, I soon learned not to see and hear everything. And parents who love their children should not be concerned if their house looks as though it is lived in, or if some dust is found occasionally on top of the refrigerator.

When we consider carefully how Benedict understood the role of discipline in the monastery, we must conclude that he was not primarily interested in a kind of military discipline which seems more concerned with appearances than with substance. Rather, he espoused an understanding of discipline that would hold monastics to the task of personal conversion. This difficult task demands the abandonment of dangerous illusions and the embracing of reality in honesty and humility. Once again, a healthy spiritual state is reached when monastics accept the reality of both their need and of God's loving presence and support.

9

Community Prayer

*"Indeed, nothing is to be preferred
to the Work of God"* (RB 43:3).

When Benedict declares the primacy of the Work of God
in the lives of monastics, he is referring to that carefully
regulated public prayer of the community to which he
devotes no less than twelve chapters in the Rule. The content of this public prayer was primarily the psalms but
there were also readings from both the Hebrew scriptures
and the New Testament. Interspersed among these biblical
passages were occasional composed prayers.

As we all know, the psalms speak frequently about God's
mighty deeds of salvation and they extol God's goodness
and mercy. Monastics are expected to respond to this
reminder of God's goodness and presence by quiet medita-
tion and prayer. However, the psalms are often prayers of
praise and gratitude themselves. In that case, the prayerful
response will be a continuation of praise in one's own
thoughts and words. In this way, there was to be a continuous dialogue between the scriptures and those who heard
them and were moved to respond.

Benedict is very careful to spell out in detail the structure
of this community prayer. He does not want it to be left to
the changeable whims and moods of individuals. This
accounts for the detailed prescriptions he gives in this
regard as he spells out exactly which psalms are to be said

at what times. Neither is Benedict wedded, however, to some strict personal order of worship, for he explicitly asserts that other arrangements are acceptable under the guidance of the superior. The important point is that there must be some clear structure to the community prayers. He seems to have the same concern that we see among people who write recipes for their favorite dishes. There may be some substitutions but the amounts are non-negotiable.

Benedict's words in this regard are worth noting: "Above all else we urge that if anyone finds this distribution of the psalms unsatisfactory, he should arrange whatever he judges better, provided that the full complement of one hundred and fifty psalms is by all means carefully maintained every week, and that the series begins anew each Sunday at Vigils. For monks who in a week's time say less than the full psalter with the customary canticles betray extreme indolence and lack of devotion in their service" (RB 18:22-24). It is clear that Benedict wants the members of the community to be nourished by a regular and substantial diet of psalms and other scriptural readings. The kind of order is not essential, but there must be order.

What effect this steady diet of scripture will have upon individual monastics will depend largely upon the quality of their faith. We have already noted that faith enables us to recognize the gift of God in all the aspects of life. The public prayer of the community will deepen the faith of the members both by reminding them of God's gracious deeds and by providing words for declaring their gratitude to God for the goodness that faith has discovered in their lives.

Accordingly, as our faith grows stronger and we are thereby enabled to discover goodness in the ever more mysterious and unpromising areas of life, we will cherish the opportunity to declare with the psalmist our praise and gratitude for all God's many blessings. As such prayerful persons, then, we will soon become basically grateful and deeply joyful people. We will still experience the hardships of life but these will remain more and more on the surface. At the center there will be a sense of wonder and gratitude, in spite of everything.

PRAYER AS HOSPITALITY

When Benedict sets aside choice periods of the day for public prayer and declares such times inviolable, he is asserting a principle that establishes a basis for that time-honored identification of Benedictines with hospitality. We have already pointed out the importance of hospitality as an expression of faith. The same principle applies when we speak of community prayer in monasteries. To reserve favorable times for such prayer is, in effect, to make room for God in one's life. This also explains why such prayers are to be chanted or recited slowly, with careful and substantial pauses, because making room for a guest in one's schedule should never be a grudging concession.

If this deliberate sacrifice of time was so important in Benedict's day, it is even more important in our own fast-paced world. Our secular society declares that "time is money," and nothing is supposed to be more important than money. When monastics become infected with this secular disease, they too begin to think that community prayer is taking up too much precious time. They will readily excuse their absence from prayer by noting that they are very busy with good works. Although even Benedict recognized that some few will need to be excused from common prayer, it should be obvious that such cases must remain truly exceptional.

This radical hospitality, by which the monastic community gladly entertains the divine presence, becomes then the basis for all other forms of hospitality. Those who show reverence and respect for God's mysterious presence among them will also be prepared to honor and respect the share of divine mystery that is found in each and every member of the community. This correlation is stated most forcefully in the first letter of John: "Those who say 'I love God,' and hate their brothers or sisters, are liars; for those who do not love a brother or sister whom they have seen cannot love God whom they have not seen" (4:20). Those who take time for God in the proper kind of prayer are, therefore, more likely to take time for their brothers and sisters and for their concerns.

THE PSALMS AS IDEAL MONASTIC PRAYER

It would be difficult to imagine a more appropriate medium for the interchange between God and the believer than the one hundred and fifty psalms of the Hebrew scriptures. For they have served as the prayer-book of Israel and Christianity for almost three thousand years. When looking for a fitting expression of the most profound and personal human sentiments, Jewish and Christian believers of all times have turned instinctively to the psalter. When we pray the psalms, therefore, we join a chorus of men and women of every time and place who have added their own witness of holiness to the already sacred text.

And yet, it is not always easy to see why the psalms have been so honored in the Judaeo-Christian tradition. They contain strange, archaic expressions and images; some of them seem too vengeful to be prayers; others are repetitious to the point of tedium. In a word, they are very human—and, like humans, they are sometimes strange and tedious and resentful. But, like humans, they can also be glorious, exuberant, soulful, and ever so tender.

Paradoxically, the psalms are most real and human when they are most aware of the reality of God. For it is only in the presence of God's goodness that creatures can dare to be completely honest and realistic. To be aware of the divine, then, is to be in touch with one's own humanity. And so the psalms express the sentiments of men and women who live close to their experience and who dare to embrace their pain and guilt as well as their joy and hope. They dare to do so because they are convinced, with the psalmist, of God's loving kindness and constant faithfulness.

In fact, the psalms are really one hundred and fifty variations on the theme of divine goodness. At times, there is the resonant, confident, joyful voice of praise and thanksgiving—for a new child, for a bountiful harvest, for health restored or guilt removed, for a mystical insight. At times, there is the plaintive, courageous cry of the sufferer—beset by illness, reduced to weakness, plagued by arrogant enemies, prostrated by calamity. But always there is a refrain of God's presence and trustworthiness. Even when complaining—and the psalter contains classic lamentations—the psalmist is affirming God's goodness simply because we do not bother to complain to someone who does not love us.

Benedict wanted his followers to be immersed in the psalms. They were expected to pray all one hundred and fifty of them every single week. Every spare moment was to be devoted to memorizing the psalms. They were to become second nature for monastics. He wanted the "music" of the psalms to enter the minds and hearts of all so that their cadences would become like a familiar tune that one cannot stop humming. We know that Benedict himself had acquired this familiarity because he wove verses of the psalms into passages of the Rule almost as if they had become part of his sub-conscious. There are in fact more than seventy references to the psalms in the Rule, and this book of the bible is easily the one most often cited by Benedict.

I have tried to think of an image that would illustrate this subtle but effective action of the psalms on the minds and hearts of those who are faithful to them. The image I have found most apt to express this mysterious action is that of the crock-pot. It cooks by a process that is very slow, quiet and unobtrusive, but it tenderizes the toughest cuts of meat in a way that is so subtle that one is invariably surprised at the result. Some may prefer the noisy, hissing pressure cooker, and it is no doubt effective too—and certainly takes less time. But that is not the Benedictine way. Benedictines have always been very patient in matters of conversion, for they are convinced that haste is not fruitful in the long run. And I suspect that many a tough-willed monastic (or other Christian) has been made docile and gentle before God by faithful praying of the psalms.

THE PSALMS AS A SOURCE OF PEACE

Where there is sincerity and good will this fidelity to the psalms will contribute to a gradual conversion from a life full of suppressed anger and self-pity to an attitude of gratefulness and a sense of wonder. Thus the psalms will work their special magic as they bring equanimity and peace into the lives of those who are plagued by impatience and subject to wild mood swings. This kind of conversion is illustrated by a story from the desert fathers.

It seems that a young and fervent monk was becoming very impatient with his apparent lack of progress in the spiritual life. And so he went to a venerable and holy *abba* to seek advice. He told the old man that he was careful to say all one hundred and fifty psalms each day as good monks are supposed to do. However, he was finding it more and more difficult to enter into the spirit of the joyful psalms on those days when he was feeling depressed, just as it was hard to pray psalms like the *Miserere* when he was himself in a jubilant mood.

The old man nodded his head in recognition of the problem. The young monk then presented his own ingenious suggestion for dealing with this difficulty. He wondered if it would not be better to say the seventy-five basically upbeat psalms twice during the week when he was in a buoyant mood and, conversely, the seventy-five basically downbeat psalms twice during the week when he felt sad and lonely. In this way, he explained, he would be able to say one hundred and fifty psalms each week and could also enter with more conviction into the spirit of the psalms he was reciting.

The old *abba* smiled and assured the young monk that, though he admired his ingenuity, it was obvious that he was very inexperienced in matters of the spirit. The old man went on then to point out that it is precisely when we are feeling low that we should be saying the "Alleluia," as a reminder that many people in the world are rejoicing in their recognition of God's blessings in their lives. And we should also realize that it is precisely when we are feeling joyful that we should be saying the more sober psalms to make us aware of the many people who that day are saddened by grief or illness.

The young monk was thus reminded by the wise *abba* that a faithful praying of the psalms will enable us to escape from a dangerously self-centered view of life as we are made aware of the reality of our place in the community of all men and women. In this way, the peaks and valleys of our moods will be leveled out and we will begin to acquire that peace and equanimity that is a hallmark of true holiness as well as a basis for psychic good health.

THE DAVID SPIRIT IN THE PSALMS

The psalms will transform the person who is faithful to them in another significant way. They will gradually wean monastics away from that immature tendency to blame others for their problems, to indulge in self-pity and to allow negative sentiments to gain more and more control over their lives. I am convinced that ancient Israel understood this power of the psalms and that they expressed this in their surprising assignment of all the psalms to King David. They knew even better than we do that David could not have written more than a dozen or so of the one hundred and fifty psalms. But they also knew that whoever wrote the psalms was a person like David, that is, a person filled with David's spirit.

David was, of course, an important historical figure in Israel but he was much more than that. The tradition granted him symbolic significance; he was portrayed there in a way that was "bigger than life." Moreover, this symbolic portrait is made clearer by contrasting it with the tragic career of David's immediate predecessor, King Saul. For if one wishes to heighten the effect of white, one simply places it against a black background. A casual reading might suggest that David was luckier than Saul or that he was the darling of the gods. But that would be a pagan explanation of their contrasting fortunes. Such a solution would be unacceptable in Israel.

A closer examination makes it quite clear that it was the quality of their *faith* that separated David from Saul. Both of them believed in God and both no doubt believed in the goodness of God. However, David, unlike Saul, believed also in the goodness of God's creation and of God's future. But, most of all, David believed in the goodness of David. He knew that God loved him and trusted him and wished him to take responsibility for his own life. Saul's faith was far too shallow for such liberating convictions. And so he worried and fretted and magnified the evil in his life until he ended in bitterness and suicide. He thus became for all time the model of failure.

By contrast, David took charge of his life, did not waste

time in fruitless complaining, repented of his rash sinfulness and was better for it. He had much sorrow in his life too. He endured incest, murder and rebellion in his own family. But he never lost sight of God's goodness and so was able to rise above all his difficulties. Indeed he was so conscious of God's presence and goodness that he deserved to be the model of Israel's future messiah. Jesus himself delighted in being called "son of David"(e.g., Mt 21:9).

This positive spirit of faith permeates the psalms and will inevitably influence those who pray them. For the psalms not only reflect real life with all its warts and wrinkles; they take us beyond that to forgiveness and compassion and invincible hope. When the young David saw the giant Goliath, he was not paralyzed by fear, as were Saul and his soldiers. They could think of fighting the giant only in the old way, with sword and spear—a way that guaranteed defeat. David discovered a new way to deal with evil and violence. Faith in God released his imagination and enabled him to remember his expertise with the slingshot. When he did so, the giant was as good as dead. Thus faith liberates from old, bankrupt ways and enables one to see the promise in unconventional methods.

And when Jesus, son of David, confronted the ultimate Goliath of sin and death, he too trusted God and found the radical new way of love and sacrifice to conquer sin and death forever. In some ways, the transfiguration of Jesus is comparable in his career to that moment when David's face brightened as he thought of the new way to slay the giant. By contrast, the Saul of the New Testament is the tragic figure of Judas, who betrayed his master and also ended his life in suicide. Every human being is confronted with a choice between David and Christ or Saul and Judas. It is very tempting to take the path of self-pity and victimhood but the result is always tragic. The psalms of David help us to remember God's goodness and to dare to choose hope and to take responsibility for our lives.

THE EVIL OF MURMURING

If there were any doubt about whether Benedict recognized this contrast between the spirit of David and that of Saul, it should be removed by a consideration of how he emphasizes the danger of a negative and grousing spirit among monastics. His words are clear and strong: "First and foremost, there must be no word or sign of the evil of murmuring, no manifestation of it for any reason at all" (my translation) (RB 34:6). And again: "Above all else we admonish (monks) to refrain from murmuring" (my translation) (RB 40:9). (I think that the *RB1980* translation, "grumbling," is too weak, for it seems to suggest little more than complaining.)

The strong words of Benedict suggest that he is referring to nothing less than that corrosive, negative talk that destroys morale in the community and perpetuates the bitterness of Saul. In many ways, this negative attitude is more dangerous than outright hostility, for it is insidious as it uses subtle suggestions to exploit the vulnerability of trusting and compassionate people. An example of this would be the apparently innocent question: "Have you noticed how bad things are recently?" A sensitive person is almost compelled to reply: "No, but now that you mention it…" Only true faith which makes God's goodness a reality in one's life can protect against such dangerous temptations.

In fact, this negative, grousing attitude can even destroy the value of obedience, as Benedict makes clear when he writes: "If a disciple obeys grudgingly and murmurs, not only aloud but also in his heart, then, even though he carries out the order, his action will not be accepted with favor by God, who sees that he is murmuring in his heart. He will have no reward for service of this kind; on the contrary, he will incur punishment for murmuring, unless he changes for the better and makes amends" (RB 5:17-19) (my translation). One can easily see why such griping is destructive of the spirit of obedience when one recalls that monastic obedience should be gladly embraced as that indispensable means for discovering the path that leads to the fulfillment of the monastic's vision.

At the same time, Benedict recognized the distinction between this kind of destructive and negative grousing and a milder form of complaining which is a way of dealing with and expressing the occasional pain of a burdensome human situation. For he tells the abbot that he "should so regulate and arrange all matters that souls may be saved and the brothers may go about their activities without justifiable grumbling" (RB 41:5). Such "justifiable" complaining would belong to the category of the psalms of lamentation which, though they are plaintive enough, never lose sight of God's goodness and mercy.

The fact remains, however, that Benedict clearly understood that a negative, Saul-like spirit is destructive of monastic joy and harmony. This is so because people who suffer from this disease are able to infect others also. In fact, this seems to be exactly what Benedict has in mind when he writes in that magnificent chapter 72 of the Rule: "Just as there is a wicked zeal of bitterness which separates from God and leads to hell, so there is a good zeal which separates from evil and leads to God and everlasting life" (vv. 1-2). No passage in the Rule demonstrates more clearly how seriously Benedict took the threat of a negative, bitter spirit among those who are pledged to be witnesses of hope in the world.

SCRIPTURE STUDY AND PRAYER

In order to draw maximum benefit from praying the psalms, we should of course use every opportunity to study them. Such study should take advantage of the best critical and scholarly studies. However, the real spiritual nourishment of the psalms, though assisted by such study, will come primarily from an absorption of the wisdom of the psalms that derives from vibrant faith and true humility. The psalms, like all the words of scripture, can speak to a level of our being that is deeper than the rational. There is no need, therefore, to understand all the words or even to agree with them. They become most beneficial when we are able to disengage our rational machinery and to open our hearts to them as they speak to us of God's reality and presence.

Modern Christians who pray the scriptures have a great advantage over Benedict and his contemporaries when it comes to discovering the literal meaning of the biblical text. We are blest today with dictionaries and commentaries which those ancients never dreamed of. However, as we pointed out in Chapter 1, when we go beyond this scholarly interpretation, we have much to learn from the ancients. For the words of scripture were written by believers for believers and, at this second stage of interpretation, those ancient monastics and fathers of the church may have a distinct advantage over us who, for all our scholarly expertise, may not measure up to their example of humility and faith.

Thomas Merton speaks to nature of this deeper interpretation which takes up where scholarship leaves off. He writes: "We bring to the Psalms the raw material of our own poor, isolated persons, with our own individual conflicts and sufferings and trials. We throw them into the fire of Christ's love....In those flames we are purified of everything that isolates us, everything that is merely private, merely our own, and we are melted down to become a 'new creature' with a new identity" (*Bread in the Wilderness*, p. 93).

Merton's reference to a "new creature" reminds us of a similar statement by St. Paul in 2 Corinthians 5:17: "So if anyone is in Christ, there is a new creation: everything old has passed away; see, everything has become new!" Such a transformation is clearly due to the power of God working in the believer.

In the present context, that power of faith works through the psalms to enable those who pray them to be united with Christ and therefore with one another. The point is that the power of God transforms such a person because of faith, not because of scholarship. Scholarly interpretation remains indispensable, and we will surely be held accountable for missed opportunities in this regard. But humility and faith are also essential and, in this respect, we are no better, and perhaps somewhat worse, than our forebears.

Thomas Merton makes another observation that will be readily appreciated by all monastics. He points out that our appreciation of the role of faith in praying the psalms "will help us to understand the importance of the choral recitation of the Divine Office. The mere fact of standing in choir and of hearing twenty or thirty or fifty or a hundred voices all blending into one voice, crying out to God in the first person singular, is a great help toward realizing the truth of our transformation under the influence of the Psalms" (*Bread in the Wilderness*, p. 93).

We should also take to heart Benedict's admonition that monastics should be more concerned with the quality of their public prayers than with their length. He writes: "In community, prayers should always be brief…" (RB 20:5). Community prayers should occupy prime time and should be sung or recited in an unhurried and careful manner but we should resist the temptation of thinking that longer is always better, or that solemn occasions demand endless ceremonies. In this matter, short and fervent is always better than long and tedious.

THE PLACE OF THE EUCHARIST
IN MONASTIC PRAYER

It is very difficult to determine exactly when the eucharist was celebrated in Benedict's monastery. It seems that the community received communion every day but attended mass only on Sundays. This has led some to conclude that the daily eucharist in contemporary monasteries is unnecessary. But such a conclusion fails to take into account a valid and fruitful development in our understanding of the eucharist in the life of Christians. This is a complex question but two observations would seem to be appropriate here.

First of all, as we have already noted, it is Christ through whom we receive the goodness of God in our lives. It is also in Christ that we return our praise and thanks to the Father. Nowhere does this happen more truly and effectively than in the eucharist in which we add our humble gifts to the perfect offering of Christ and thus are assured that they will be pleasing to the Father. Our participation in the body and blood of the Lord helps us to appreciate the degree of God's love for us as it also assists us in our task of making that goodness and love available to all whom we meet.

This is so central to the meaning of all the scriptures that it is hard to believe that daily celebration could be excessive. In fact, just as the psalms once celebrated the goodness of the God of the exodus, so do they now enable us to celebrate the wonders of God revealed in the new exodus of the passion, death and resurrection of Jesus. In the liturgy of the hours, therefore, monastics are preparing for the ultimate praise of the eucharist which in turn takes them to the timeless heart of God's work of salvation among us.

Secondly, when we realize how much less time is now devoted to the liturgy of the hours than was the case in Benedict's day, and when we note how much of the eucharist is made up of biblical readings and commentary, it seems that one can make a very good case for seeing the eucharist as an integral part of the public prayer of monasteries. It would help also to have the monastic eucharist more effectively declericalized, not through the elimination of concelebration, but through a down-playing of the more divisive features of that practice.

In any case, the public prayer of the monastery should be recognized as a spiritual leaven that works on the community, slowly but surely, to make it a congregation of grateful people, filled with a desire to share its blessings with the whole world. The same effect can be achieved by non-monastic Christians who attempt to reserve precious time in their daily schedule for praying the psalms or in other ways attending to the Lord.

Although Christians who do not live in a monastery will not have the opportunity to participate daily in common prayer, they will nonetheless be able to find moments here and there for reciting the prayers in a short breviary or for simply praying the psalms. In this way, they will be able to join in spirit that centuries-old tradition of monastic prayer. And they will also benefit richly from it in the same way that monastics do.

10

Personal or Private Prayer

"...let (the monk) recall that he is always seen
by God in heaven" (RB 7:13).

St. Benedict takes it for granted that his followers will
want to pray in a more personal and private manner outside the common, public prayer of the Divine Office. We
recall that he refers specifically to this kind of prayer when
he writes: "Moreover, if at other times someone chooses to
pray privately, he may simply go in (to the oratory) and
pray, not in a loud voice, but with tears and heartfelt devotion" (RB 52:4). And, among the Instruments for Good
Works, he urges the monk "to devote himself often to
prayer" (RB 4:56).

PRAYER AS AWARENESS OF GOD'S PRESENCE

When we look more closely at Benedict's concept of private prayer, however, we begin to realize that it is not identical with our own idea of such prayer. We would probably
describe private prayer as a setting aside of some time for
quiet reflection and adoration. It would be a kind of island
of serenity in a sea of turbulent daily concerns. For Benedict,
such prayer would certainly include this kind of explicit and
conscious attention to the Lord. However, it would not be
limited to such special moments of recollection.

A careful reading of the Rule makes it clear that Benedict wished his monastic followers to make the entire day a time of more or less intense awareness of God's presence. Such an awareness may indeed wax or wane, but ideally it will never be totally absent as the monastic learns to bask in the warmth of that presence and to celebrate it with grateful thoughts. In a word, Benedict wished his followers to be not just people who prayed occasionally, but quite simply prayerful people. Accordingly, we should consider those texts of the Rule that refer to the monastic's awareness of the divine presence as in fact texts about personal prayer.

It is remarkable how often Benedict does in fact remind monastics of the enveloping presence of God in their lives. He writes, for example: "...let (the monk) recall that he is always seen by God in heaven, (and) that his actions everywhere are in God's sight and are reported by angels at every hour" (RB 7:13). We should note the word "recall" in this text because Benedict is surely not merely stating a theological fact about the omnipresence of God. Rather, he wishes monastics to recall or be conscious of this fact in their personal experience. The text is not about God seeing everyone but about everyone knowing that he or she is seen by God.

Nor is this an isolated comment by Benedict. He is insistent on this point, as is clear from other texts in the Rule. He writes in chapter 4, for example: "Hour by hour keep careful watch over all you do, aware that God's gaze is upon you wherever you may be" (RB 4:48-49). And again, in chapter 7: "The first step of humility, then, is that a man keeps the 'fear of God' always 'before his eyes' (Ps 36:2) and never forgets it" (RB 7:10). When we recall, as noted earlier, that humility represents an acceptance of reality, it becomes clear why Benedict judges the basis of humility to be an acknowledgement of the primary reality of God's presence everywhere.

To be a prayerful person, whether lay or monastic, means therefore to avoid becoming so engrossed in one's work or play that one is not gently "distracted" by the awareness of God's gracious and loving presence. The fact that this is an ideal for all believers, and not just for monastics, is evident from the frequent emphasis on this ideal in the scriptures.

"HEAR, O ISRAEL" (Dt 6:4)

The unparalleled importance of a prayerful awareness of God's reality and presence is signaled by that powerful statement which has come to be known as the primary act of faith for Israel. "Hear, O Israel: The Lord is our God, the Lord alone. You shall love the Lord your God with all your heart, and with all your soul, and with all your might. Keep these words that I am commanding you today in your heart. Recite them to your children and talk about them when you are at home and when you are away, when you lie down and when you rise. Bind them as a sign on your hand, fix them as an emblem on your forehead, and write them on the doorposts of your house and on your gates" (Dt 6:4-9).

This remarkable admonition not only reminds Israel of the undivided loyalty owed to the God who alone delivered them from bondage but it also challenges them to give this gracious God the primary place in their minds and hearts. In fact, to be in touch with reality means to be constantly aware of the very center of reality which is the existence and all-enveloping presence of God who is far more real and present than the air we breathe or the objects we touch or even the bodies which house our spirits. It is only natural then that such an awareness should be "in our hearts," that is, present to our deepest sense of being and living. This is reality; all else is partial or total illusion.

And because the reality of God's presence is central to the very meaning of our lives, we will instinctively want to share this treasure with those whom we love. It will be the first and constant message that parents give to their children. In the case of monastics, it is probably the most significant element in their witnessing to the church and to the world. For what could be more beneficial than to remind busy and distracted people of the reality of God's presence—a presence that will survive all the human turmoil of living and dying?

In order to prevent this awareness from being eroded by the cares and concerns of life, the scriptures urge us to surround ourselves with reminders of this gracious, life-giving presence. Remembering to love the Lord must be as familiar as the movement of one's hand or the glance of one's eye. Even the doorpost will bear witness to those who enter and exit the home. The clear implication is that, even in our busiest and most engrossing moments, we will never be altogether forgetful of God's goodness. In fact, the reality of the divine presence will be a kind of constant distraction so that we will occasionally smile, without apparent cause, as people are accustomed to do when they are in love.

"WE BELIEVE THAT THE DIVINE PRESENCE IS EVERYWHERE" (RB 19:1)

Benedict does not refer directly to the text just quoted from Deuteronomy, but the message of that text is found everywhere in the Rule. Benedict is explicit on this point: "We believe that the divine presence is everywhere and 'that in every place the eyes of the Lord are watching the good and the wicked' (Prv 15:3)" (RB 19:1). And a few verses later he writes: "Let us consider, then, how we ought to behave in the presence of God and his angels..." (RB 19:6).

Benedict stresses the importance of God's presence when he speaks, in chapter 7, about humility: "(The monk) must constantly remember everything God has commanded, keeping in mind that all who despise God will burn in hell for their sins, and all who fear God have everlasting life awaiting them. While he guards himself at every moment from sins and vices of thought or tongue, of hand or foot, of self-will or bodily desire, let him recall that he is always seen by God in heaven, that his actions everywhere are in God's sight and are reported by angels at every hour" (RB 7:11-13).

Nor is this presence of God to the monastic to be understood simply as a kind of divine companionship. Benedict writes, in the same chapter 7: "The Prophet indicates (the fact of God's presence) to us when he shows that God is *always present to our thoughts*, saying: 'God searches hearts and minds' (Ps 7:10)" (RB 7:14) (emphasis added). God is pictured, therefore, as present to the innermost recesses of mind and heart.

We may become masters at hiding our true feelings from other human beings, but nothing is hidden from God. This fact can be frightening or consoling. As we grow in genuine self-knowledge and trust in the Lord, consolation will gradually replace fear. We will learn to accept our human frailty and to allow God's power to work through it. Benedict suggests as much when he writes: "As for the desires of the body, we must believe that God is always with us, for 'All my desires are known to you' (Ps 38:10)" (RB 7:23). It is in fact both impossible and unnecessary to hide anything from God.

"WE MUST BE VIGILANT EVERY HOUR" (RB 7:29)

In the same chapter on humility, Benedict touches upon the one indispensable element in a prayerful life, namely, constant attention to the Lord. He writes: "Accordingly, if 'the eyes of the Lord are watching the good and the wicked' (Prv 15:3), if at all times 'the Lord looks down from heaven on the sons of men to see whether any understand and seek God' (Ps 14:2), and if every day the angels assigned to us report our deeds to the Lord day and night, then, brothers, we must be vigilant every hour…" (RB 7:26-29). To be "vigilant every hour" means nothing less than to be constantly aware of God's reality and presence.

Such vigilance is not so much a fearful watching as it is a confident awareness of the reality of God's goodness. In this case, watching is opposed to a distracted and forgetful state. We find this expressed most clearly in the gospel story about the experience of Jesus in the garden of Gethsemane. After having confronted the terrors of imminent death, Jesus returned to his sleeping disciples and said to them: "Keep awake and pray" (Mk 14:38). They are pictured asleep because they are not yet, like Jesus, experiencing the final moment, but their time will come. In the meantime, they must be vigilant and prayerful. In fact, Jesus could just as easily have said, "Keep awake; that is, pray."

To watch by praying is to be ever mindful of God's place in one's life. In the context of Gethsemane, Jesus is telling his disciples that their only hope of facing death without fear is to be conscious every day of God's loving presence so that they too, like himself, will be able to say, "Father…not what I want but what you want" (Mt 26:39). In other words, we as well as the disciples are admonished to give God a choice place in our busy lives so that in the final hour God will be with us, not as a stranger, but as a familiar and trusted friend.

We know that this admonition to be vigilant is found also in those passages of the gospel that warn us to be ready for the coming of the Lord. A typical example is the passage in Mark: "Be on your guard, keep watch. You do not know when the moment is coming" (13:33). Monastics have been especially sensitive to this admonition. Their night office has been called "vigils" because they are thought to be watching and praying in preparation for the coming of the Lord. Indeed, they have always thought of themselves as representatives of all other men and women in this prayerful watching.

PURITY OF HEART

To be prayerfully attentive to the Lord is to be free, not only of external distractions, but also of those powerful internal tendencies which the early monastics called "passions." They are not limited to strong emotions. Rather, they are all those influences which distort reality. Roberta Bondi has written beautifully on this subject: "A passion is a strong emotion or state of mind that blinds the one whom it possesses, making it impossible to see anything, or anyone, even God, as it really is" (*To Love as God Loves*, p. 106). Thus, anger is a passion, but so is lethargy.

To be "pure of heart" is to be basically free of the influence of the passions. Purity of heart is intimately connected with prayer because freedom from the passions means that one is free to be attentive to the Lord. Benedict was well aware of this and pointed out that the quality of our prayer is more important than its quantity: "We must know that God regards our purity of heart and tears of compunction, not our many words. Prayer should therefore be short and pure..." (RB 20:3-4).

Michael Casey is especially helpful on this point. He notes that purity of heart begins with a simple renunciation of sinfulness and then progresses to the gradual elimination of sinful tendencies. Finally, even the imagination is brought into harmony with one's focus on God. He writes: "In this state the monk is substantially free of distractions; prayer comes readily and often, but it is so in tune with the monk's entire subjectivity that he scarcely notices its presence. Pure prayer, mentioned three times in RB 20, is simply prayer which proceeds naturally from an undivided heart, fully possessed by charity" (*The Undivided Heart,* p. 29).

"IN THE PRESENCE OF GOD AND HIS ANGELS"
(RB 19:6)

Benedict's emphasis on prayer as an awareness of God's presence is reflected also in his frequent reference to angels. This presupposes a biblical understanding of the role of angels, namely, that they serve as intermediaries between us humans and our transcendent God. They thus make it possible for God to be truly present or immanent to human history without compromising divine majesty or transcendence. Accordingly, when one wishes to emphasize the omnipresence of God, one simply fills the world with angels.

In later tradition, this role of mediation has been taken over to a large extent by the Blessed Virgin and the saints, but the angels have enjoyed in recent years an unprecedented popularity. It should be noted that this need for mediators is felt especially when our emphasis on the divinity of Christ is strong, and that has been the case ever since the Arian heresy. Mediators will always be needed but their importance will be stressed more or less as perceptions change. For the bible and for Benedict, the role of mediation belonged, after Christ, primarily to the angels.

PRAYER AS BENIGN DISTRACTION

If it is possible to see one's awareness of God's presence as a kind of constant distraction, one may wonder whether this does not endanger proper attention to one's work which, in many cases, requires very close attention. My own judgment is that one should make a distinction between dangerous distractions, which scatter one's attention, and benign distractions which actually enable one to focus more intensely and peacefully on the work at hand. To be conscious of God's loving presence is so connatural and wholesome that it actually serves to integrate one's psychic powers which are otherwise constantly in danger of dissipation.

An example from everyday life may illustrate this point. A mother working at a hot stove or a father using a dangerous piece of equipment is not likely to be endangered by glancing momentarily at her or his child playing nearby and smiling briefly with love and gratitude. The same would be true of a teacher or pastor or even an author who pauses for a moment to think of God's love and of his or her share in it.

The really dangerous distractions, by contrast, are those which arise from such attitudes as anger and resentment or a negative spirit. Such feelings may derive from an excessive concern about approval or smoldering resentment at perceived mistreatment or angry impatience and frustration at a seeming lack of success. And all of these situations reveal a lack of awareness of God's love and a consequent excessive dependence on one's own resources.

The love and affirmation of other human beings is a major source of blessing in anyone's life. However, even the best humans are sometimes fickle and inconstant. To rely solely on their affection is to risk living on a kind of roller coaster that takes one to the heights of euphoria and to the depths of aloneness. A deep awareness of God's loving presence reduces this excessive dependence on other creatures. They remain very important but their approval is no longer indispensable for one's happiness.

We know, of course, that only God can satisfy the deepest yearnings of our hearts. It is basically unfair, therefore, to ask any human being to meet that need. And when we do place such unrealistic expectations on our friends, we are likely to drive them away or at least to make them feel very uncomfortable. No one likes to be asked to play God. The really healthy situation is to feel deeply affirmed by God's loving presence and to be free to accept gratefully human affirmation also, without however being desperate for it.

PRAYER AS ATTENTION TO THE LORD

Society was in turmoil at the time of Benedict. The great Roman empire had collapsed and various foreign armies were struggling to control the remnants of it. However, it is unlikely that the distractions of those days were more pervasive than those which we experience today. Even the most private places are invaded by television and radio. In such situations, the serious Christian must find a way to shut out the noise in order to become aware of God's presence. This can happen only through special periods of intense personal prayer.

These periods of personal prayer need not be long but they must be regular. In praying, as in dieting or exercising, to binge is not helpful. Benedict seems to have had something like this in mind when he wrote: "...every time you begin a good work, you must pray to (God) most earnestly to bring it to perfection" (Prol 4), or when he lists among the Instruments for Good Works the command: "...devote yourself often to prayer" (RB 4:56). Benedict does not discuss the nature of these moments of prayer interspersed throughout the day, but we can assume that they were brief and intense recollections of the divine presence.

In fact, these prayerful moments may very well have been similar to the prayer of quiet or of listening which was well known in monastic circles and was mentioned by Benedict's predecessor, John Cassian. In such moments of recollection, one simply says to the Lord: "Tell me what I need to know," and then becomes very quiet and attentive, immersed as it were in God's deeply experienced presence. Such periods of total attention to the Lord become special moments of grace which radiate into the intervening times of one's busy life to produce a deep calm and serenity that will make all the difference.

In a very real sense, this kind of prayer is the ultimate expression of that "listening" which is an indispensable element of monastic life. It is no accident that Benedict begins his Rule with the word "listen," and that this attitude is at the heart of monastic obedience. But beyond the disciple's attentiveness to the superior's words is a deeper sensitivity to the presence of God. To be attentive in this sense is to rise above self-absorption so that one can focus on the only real source of freedom. The consequence will be a deep calm that cannot be disturbed by any surface turmoil, not even by personal illness or tragedy.

MONASTIC HOSPITALITY

Such attentiveness to the Lord not only approximates the ancient ideal of continuous prayer but it is also an exercise in that radical monastic hospitality that entertains or makes room for God's presence in one's life. During my student days in Rome I recall vividly the words of a venerable professor, Father Matthaeus, who insisted that the essence of monastic witness is expressed in the words *vacare Deo*, that is, "to make room for God."

In both unhurried public prayer and the attentiveness of private prayer, therefore, monastics center their lives in the entertainment of God's loving presence. As we noted earlier, if monastics have a reputation for hospitality it is first of all because they are hospitable toward God's mystery. For hospitality means making room for a stranger, and the ultimate stranger is that deep mystery of God's being. Abraham illustrated this when he welcomed the strangers at Mamre (Gn 18), as did also the two disciples on the road to Emmaus (Lk 24:13f). The classic way to entertain God's mystery is through prayer. And, as in all cases of hospitality, the welcome must be personal and unhurried.

Hospitality to other human beings and respect for their mystery flows naturally out of this deep reverence for God's presence. This loving respect is shown first of all to the other members of the monastic community. It will be a love that is very personal but not possessive. As Benedict himself notes, "To their fellow monks they will show the pure love of brothers" (RB 72:8). Above all, they will avoid the familiarity that breeds contempt or that causes others to feel excluded.

This authentic hospitality will overflow the community and offer loving service to guests, to students in the monastic school and to all God's people in whatever ministry monastics may undertake. Particularly important beneficiaries of this kind of hospitality have been all those who over the centuries have benefited from the missionary zeal of Benedictine monks and nuns. It must be noted, of course, that the energy for all this outreach is that quiet, unhurried prayer that is the heart and soul of monastic life.

Finally, the same loving respect will embrace all of material creation as well. The monastic instinct has always been very respectful toward the mystery that the creator has placed in even the most insignificant creatures. Over the centuries, monastics have been known for their care of the environment. They were concerned about ecology long before it became fashionable to be so. Medieval monasteries and convents were centers, not only for education, but also for developing the art of agriculture. They were famous for fine beers and wines. And they were devoted to art, music and architecture. Material creation was for them filled with a beauty that asked only to be released. In this sense, their work too was prayer.

Benedict provides a simple but telling example of this concern for inanimate creation when he orders the cellarer to "regard all utensils and goods of the monastery as sacred vessels of the altar…" (RB 31:10), or when he reminds all monastic laborers to show respect for their tools: "Whoever fails to keep the things belonging to the monastery clean or treats them carelessly should be reproved" (RB 32:4). The watchword is respect, and the motivation is love of God's creation.

In a sense, Benedict sums up this prayerful notion of hospitality when he emphasizes the proper use of the time that God has entrusted to us. He writes in the Prologue: "If we wish to reach eternal life, even as we avoid the torments of hell, then—while there is still time, while we are in this body, and have time to accomplish all these things by the light of life—we must run and do now what will profit us forever" (vv. 42-44). What will profit us forever is, more than anything else, a life that is marked by prayerful reverence and gratitude.

11

Mystical Intimations

"Let us open our eyes to the deifying light..." (Prol 9).

The Rule of Benedict would probably not be considered a major source for mystical theology. We find very little there about mystical experience. However, there are hints or intimations of mysticism everywhere. After all, union with Christ is at the center of Benedict's spirituality, and that is, of course, the essential element in Christian mysticism. The difference is that Benedict espouses living in a mystical way without talking much about it.

Benedict may have chosen to be reticent about mystical language because of heretical tendencies in his day when neo-Platonism, channeled through Origen and Evagrius of Pontus, was still a powerful influence. Or he may have simply shared the church's perennial concern lest mysticism degenerate into pantheism or tend to compromise the importance of the communitarian and sacramental life of the church. At the same time, there is an orientation in Benedict's spirituality that points toward a mystical fruition that is both exemplary and orthodox.

FACING THE FUTURE WITH CHRIST

This mystical orientation can be seen, first of all, in Benedict's adoption of the vision of scripture concerning the powerful magnetism that draws all of human history toward the end of time, thereby recognizing the primacy of *promise* as a basic element in biblical revelation. It is true that God has entered history in a new way in the person of Jesus and that God's presence thereby permeates every moment of time. But Jesus rose from the dead and, in a very real sense, went into the radical future to the bosom of the Father who, from that radical future, called his Son and now all of us to himself.

The Spirit was sent by the risen Lord to convince us in our deepest being of God's love for us, but also to make us ache with yearning to finish the journey and to join Jesus with the Father. In fact, the Spirit dwells in us, not only to comfort us, but also to make us homesick. St. Paul says as much when he writes: "And because you are children, God has sent the Spirit of his Son in our hearts, crying, 'Abba! Father'" (Gal 4:6). To be a mystic in the biblical tradition is, therefore, to be profoundly sensitive to this presence of God in the most ordinary events of life but, at the same time, to be aware that this divine presence is constantly calling us to the radical future. This is that bitter-sweet experience that has made the Song of Solomon a perennial favorite of mystics.

Monastics have always appreciated this dynamic and future-oriented meaning of the gospel and have made it their hallmark in relation to all other Christians. Benedict was in the full stream of this tradition. We recall the stirring words of the Prologue: "What, dear brothers, is more delightful than this voice of the Lord calling to us? See how the Lord in his love shows us the way of life. With loins girded then by faith and the performance of good works, let us set out on this way, with the gospel for our guide, that we may deserve to see him 'who has called us to his kingdom' (1 Thes 2:12)" (vv. 19-21) (my translation). And, among the Tools for Good Works, we find the earnest admonition: "Yearn for everlasting life with holy desire"

(RB 4:46). Finally, at the end of the Rule, Benedict asks: "Are you hastening toward your heavenly home? Then with Christ's help, keep this little rule that we have written for beginners" (RB 73:8).

All these texts strongly suggest that monastics will not only enter upon the journey of conversion because of an initial glimpse of the transcendent One but that, as they pursue their ideals with good will and sincerity, they will find that the motivation for their perseverance will come more and more from the future, illuminated as it is by God's promise. This will result in a gradual liberation from the need to look toward past accomplishments or present assurances for confidence and a sense of personal well-being. Benedict clearly states as much when he concludes his long and important chapter on humility with these words: "Now, therefore, after ascending all these steps of humility, the monk will quickly arrive at that 'perfect love' of God which 'casts out fear' (1 Jn 4:18). Through this love, all that he once performed with dread, he will now begin to observe without effort, as though naturally, from habit, no longer out of fear of hell, but out of love for Christ, good habit and delight in virtue" (RB 7:67-69).

It is not, therefore, out of fear of the prospect of future punishment but out of sure hope of future glory with the Lord that monastics will now "run the way of God's commandments" (Prol 49). I have often thought that an apt image for this transformation, from a secular fear of the ultimate future to the believer's yearning for it, is that of a small child learning to walk. When the little one begins that first perilous journey from one parent across the room to the other, it will at first look back to the nearest parent for encouragement. However, at a critical moment near the middle of the adventure, the child will put out its arms and hurry toward the parent who is awaiting it. In much the same way, when faith begins to be truly victorious in our lives, we will begin to actually draw more comfort from the assurance of a loving God awaiting us than from the fading memories of past accomplishments. This should be true for all Christians but doubly so for monastics.

And so we note that it is precisely when the secular vision of life, based on human strength and control, proves illusory and deceptive that the monastic vision comes into its own. For this vision is based on God's promise and is nourished, not by a sense of personal autonomy, but by the experience of divine love. It is the strange and wonderful paradox of greater joy and confidence precisely when everything seems out of control. From a secular perspective, the prospect of becoming more and more dependent on others as age and disease take their toll is daunting, to say the least. And it is especially difficult for those who have prided themselves on their self-reliance. But, for true believers, and above all for monastics, this is a time to live serenely, or at least cheerfully, in trust and patience. For there is the sure knowledge of God's love which they have already learned to recognize as the only valid guarantee of security. Such a hopeful vision is surely at the heart of mystical intuition.

SHARING IN CHRIST'S TRANSFIGURATION

It is important to insist upon the fact that such a faith-filled and happy ending to human life is not a matter of some superficial overlay of piety or ritual. We hear frequently about various apparitions and, though they may be helpful reminders of God's concern for us, they cannot replace the daily struggle of conversion. Moreover, such conversion happens only where one has become so identified with Christ in sincere love and gratitude that it amounts to nothing less than mystical union.

Indeed, it is this profoundly personal identification with Christ that enables a Christian believer to experience the same journey that Jesus experienced in his human nature. For, in the public ministry of Jesus, as it is described in the synoptic gospels, the critical moment occurred when it became evident that Jesus' mission of salvation was not to be accomplished by means of spectacular miracles or by challenging demons or by some other messianic tour de force. Rather, he would make God's saving power effective in the world simply by loving and sacrificing to the end. This seemingly least promising way turns out to be the only way.

It seems clear to me that the synoptic evangelists, having evaluated the public ministry of Jesus in the brilliant light of the resurrection, recognized that a critical moment had occurred in their master's life when he suddenly seemed to see the purpose of it all and then hurried toward Jerusalem. In that holy city, he found the opportunity to express his love in ultimate sacrifice, thereby letting go of all semblance of human control and entrusting himself entirely to the love and will of his heavenly Father. This critical turning point in the ministry of Jesus is signaled by that dramatic moment, at least partially symbolic in nature, which we call the transfiguration.

Since this was a moment of mystical enlightenment, it was foreordained that it should happen on a mountain top. Moses and Elijah were there to emphasize the importance of the occasion but also because they too experienced mystical revelation on a mountain top, namely, Mount Sinai (Horeb) (see Ex 19:16ff and 1 Kgs 19:8ff). In the case of Jesus, such an ecstatic moment of discovery would have been experienced in that human consciousness which he shares with all of us.

We have already noted that nothing in the gospels is presented simply to tell us about the private life of Jesus. Rather, everything recorded there is intended to teach us how to find salvation in Jesus. This means that we must also share with Jesus his transfiguring experience. Such an experience will always be in some sense mystical, for it will expose the illusion of salvation through merely human power as it reveals the power of God working through our feeble human love and trust and sacrifice to give us a freedom we cannot even imagine. To know that truth is already a mystical experience of the first order. In fact, to be enlightened in this way is to be fully united with Jesus in mystical union and to be ready for a serene and happy death.

Of course, all of this applies to the life of every Christian believer. However, it seems almost self-evident that this experience of mystical transformation is the ultimate expression of the monastic ideal. In fact, monastics render their primary and most beneficial service to humankind by witnessing to the possibility of such a victory in our fragile human nature. The serenity achieved through such a union with Christ must surely be the basis for the special claim of Benedictines to the motto, "Peace." And why else would Benedict be called the patron of a happy death except that he found and taught the secret of living so close to Christ that death itself becomes simply the last and best opportunity to trust God?

THE SINAI EXPERIENCE

When we allow for mystical intimations in the Rule, we also find new depths of meaning in a celebrated text from the Prologue: "Let us get up then, at long last, for the scriptures rouse us when they say: 'It is high time for us to arise from sleep' (Rom 13:11). Let us *open our eyes to the deifying light* and *with thunderstruck ears* let us hear the divine voice that every day calls out this charge: 'If today you hear his voice, harden not your hearts' (Ps 95:8)" (vv. 8-10) (my translation; emphasis added).

I believe that the *RB1980* translation of *deificum lumen* as "the light that comes from God" does not do justice to the more active meaning of that Latin adjective. A better translation would be, I think, "deifying" or "divinizing." This is, in fact, the conclusion of several respected translators of the Rule (see Pawlowsky, *Die Biblischen Grundlagen der Regula Benedicti*, 46). The mystical implications of such a translation should be fairly obvious, for an enlightenment that divinizes reflects a fairly common theme in the mystical tradition.

Furthermore, the *RB1980* translation of *attonitis auribus* as "open...our ears" is not at all adequate. For *attonitis* suggests "thunder" or, metaphorically, "astonishment." The connection with thunder is especially significant in a text that already has mystical possibilities because it is reminiscent of Mount Sinai, the classic biblical location for theophany and the mystical experience of divine majesty. "Now Mount Sinai was wrapped in smoke, because the Lord had descended upon it in fire...As the blast of the trumpet grew louder and louder, Moses would speak and God would answer him in thunder" (Ex 19:18-19).

Therefore, when Benedict urges us to arise from the sleep of the unenlightened or distracted ones, and to recognize the brilliant light of God's challenging presence, he seems to be inviting us to experience with Jesus nothing less than that wonderful moment of transfiguration. And the thunder of Sinai is meant to awaken us, as it did Moses and Elijah, to hear the only message that really matters—a message that is now made incarnate in the life and words of Jesus.

This is the splendid prospect that God has offered to all Christians. Monastics simply feel called to demonstrate, in quiet and patient ways, that there is real joy in this journey with Christ, for he is "the pioneer and perfecter of our faith, who for the sake of the joy that was set before him endured the cross, disregarding its shame, and has taken his seat at the right hand of the throne of God" (Heb 12:2). To be united with Christ means to see the joy that God has set before us and to be able therefore to endure whatever trials life may bring. To have one's eyes shining with the light of that anticipated joy is to know the meaning of mystical experience.

Bibliography

Bondi, Roberta. *To Love as God Loves.* Philadelphia: Fortress Press, 1987.

Brown, Raymond. *The Gospel According to John*, AB. 2 vols. Garden City, NY: Doubleday, 1966, 1970.

Burton-Christie, Douglas. *The Word in the Desert.* New York: Oxford University Press, 1993.

Casey, Michael. *The Undivided Heart.* Petersham, MA: St. Bede's Publications, 1994.

DeVogue, Adalbert. *Reading Saint Benedict: Reflections on the Rule.* Kalamazoo, MI: Cistercian Publications, 1994.

DeWaal, Esther. *Living with Contradiction: Reflections on the Rule of Saint Benedict.* San Francisco: Harper and Row, 1989.

Dumm, Demetrius. *Flowers in the Desert: A Spirituality of the Bible.* Mahwah, NJ: Paulist Press, 1987.

———. "Passover and Eucharist." *Worship* 61 (1987): 199-208.

Gomez, Ildefonso. *Regla del Maestro—Regla de S. Benito.* Zamora: Ediciones Monte Casino, 1988.

Merton, Thomas. *Bread in the Wilderness*. New York: New Directions, 1953.

Newman, John. *Historical Sketches*, II. New York: Longmans, Green and Co., 1917.

Osiek, Carolyn. "Paul's Prayer." In *Scripture and Prayer*. Edited by Carolyn Osiek and Donald Senior. Wilmington, DE: Michael Glazier, 1988.

Pawlowsky, Sigismund. *Die Biblischen Grundlagen der Regula Benedicti*. Vienna: Herder, 1965.

Pontifical Biblical Commission. *The Interpretation of the Bible in the Church*. Washington, DC: U.S. Catholic Conference, 1993.

RB1980: The Rule of Saint Benedict. Edited by Timothy Fry. Collegeville, MN: Liturgical Press, 1981.

Schneiders, Sandra. *The Revelatory Text*. San Francisco: HarperSan Francisco, 1991.

Williams, Charles. *The Greater Trumps*. New York: Farrar, Strauss and Cudahy, 1950.

Zimmermann, Odo. "The Regula Magistri: The Primitive Rule of St. Benedict." *American Benedictine Review* 1 (1950): 11-36.

Index of Biblical References

Index of References
from the Rule of Benedict

Phil Giumietto
from Fr. Carl T.